Rock & Pop

Rock & Pop

Paul Roland

TEACH YOURSELF BOOKS

For UK orders: please contact Bookpoint Ltd, 78 Milton Park, Abingdon, Oxon OX14 4TD. Telephone: (44) 01235 400414, Fax: (44) 01235 400454. Lines are open from 9.00 to 6.00, Monday to Saturday, with a 24-hour message answering service. Email address: orders@bookpoint.co.uk

For USA & Canada orders: please contact NTC/Contemporary Publishing Company, 4255 West Touhy Avenue, Lincolnwood, Illinois 60646–1975, USA. Telephone: (847) 679 5500, Fax: (847) 679 2494.

Long renowned as the authoritative source for self-guided learning – with more than 40 million copies sold worldwide – the 'Teach Yourself' series includes over 200 titles in the fields of languages, crafts, hobbies, business and education.

British Library Cataloguing in Publication Data
A catalogue entry for this title is available from The British Library.

Library of Congress Catalog Card Number: On file

First published in UK 1999 by Hodder Headline Plc, 338 Euston Road, London NW1 3BH.

First published in USA 1999 by NTC/Contemporary Publishing Company, 4255 West Touhy Avenue, Lincolnwood (Chicago), Illinois 60646–1975, USA.

The 'Teach Yourself' name and logo are registered trademarks of Hodder & Stoughton Ltd.

Copyright © 1999 Paul Roland

Typeset by Transet Limited, Coventry, England.
Printed in Great Britain for Hodder & Stoughton Educational, a division of Hodder Headline Plc, 338 Euston Road, London NW1 3BH by Cox & Wyman Ltd, Reading, Berkshire.

Impression number   10 9 8 7 6 5 4 3 2 1
Year   2005 2004 2003 2002 2001 2000 1999

This book is affectionately dedicated to my band: Derek Heffernan, John Tracey, Simon Jeffries, Chris Randall, Piers Mortimer and Jenny Benwell, who helped me to make my own small contribution to the following story.

CONTENTS

FOREWORD

I used to believe that the only aspects of rock and pop music that could be taught were the practical aspect of playing an instrument and the techniques of recording. But then when I began to write this book I discovered that being encouraged to fine tune my ears to the intricacies of even the most familiar songs intensified the enjoyment and invariably revealed nuances that I had been previously unaware of. It is not an exaggeration to say that it was almost as if I was hearing some of these classic records for the first time.

Whether you are new to popular music or can boast a library of recordings to rival the BBC, I hope and believe that this book will guide you through the confusion of categories and shelves of CDs to make similar satisfying (re)discoveries.

Of course, an overview of this length cannot promise to be comprehensive. In the first 50 years of post-war popular music there have been at least 1,000 major artists and tens of thousands of artistically and historically significant recordings which would fill several volumes if I was to give them the space that they deserve. Instead, for practical purposes I have outlined the main themes and described the important developments of each decade at the beginning of each chapter. Having set the scene, so to speak, I have confined myself to concise profiles of the artists who made a significant impact on the evolution of the music (rather than those who were the most commercially successful) and have reappraised a representative selection of classic albums which marked a high point in the history of rock and pop.

I have endeavoured to keep biographical details to an absolute minimum and have concentrated instead on conveying an impression of the personality behind the music as far as space will allow. Some of the classic album entries also help to cover those artists whose careers were erratic and can be best represented by a single release. But I should point out that the recommended recordings at the end of each chapter are equally essential. Assuming that you like the sound of the music from my description you can take it that it is safe to buy all of the albums without a second thought!

Despite my initial reservations, I took the 'Teach Yourself' tag seriously and included in each chapter a 'soundbite' in which I analyse an important recording. I guarantee that you will never listen to 'Ballroom Blitz' by The Sweet in quite the same way again!

Finally, I make no apologies for the style of writing that some might call 'journalese'. In 20 years of earning my living as a feature writer and reviewer for the British music press I find that the most effective way to convey the almost indefinable quality of popular music is to cut the clichés and go for the jugular. Or as Little Richard expressed it so eloquently, 'Awopbopaloobop Alopbamboom!'

Happy listening.

1 | GOOD ROCKIN' TONIGHT – THE ROOTS OF ROCK – THE 1950S

Origins

It is a popular misconception, one which grew into one of the most enduring myths of the twentieth century, that rock music began with Bill Haley's multimillion selling hit 'Rock Around The Clock' in 1955. While it is certainly true that Haley, a one-time country singer, helped to popularize rock and roll, he did it by diluting it to such an extent that his records are now seen as being only of historical importance. Haley was already middle-aged when he made his breakthrough and he would have been the first to admit that his sound and style were contrived; cribbed from black rhythm and blues (R&B) records which had been denied exposure on national radio and television on racial grounds. By contrast Elvis Presley, Eddie Cochran, Little Richard, Chuck Berry and the other true pioneers of pop who followed in Haley's wake were not much older than their fans and they had a genuine feeling for the music.

The roots of rock and pop music go far deeper than Haley, deeper even than the prototype 'race records' recorded by black American R&B artists in the 1940s or the hillbilly boogie and Western swing songs performed by white country musicians in the 1930s, which Haley reworked.

The roots of rock and pop were planted in the fertile soil of the southern states of America in the latter years of the nineteenth century by the European settlers and the African slaves. By the early 1920s black Negro spirituals and the so-called 'rocking and reeling' call-and-response hymns from the black Holy Roller Sanctified Churches had cross-fertilized with the white narrative folk-ballad tradition to create the first rumblings of a new African–American music. Its first blossoming was heard in the bitter-sweet beauty of the blues.

Robert Johnson (b.1911? d.1938)

They used to call the blues 'the devil's music' and for good reason. According to an enduring legend among the black community of the Mississippi Delta, any musician with a burning hunger to become one of the immortals could go to the crossroads at Highway 61 and Highway 8 at midnight and offer his guitar to Legba – more commonly known as the devil. If Legba took a shine to the musician he'd tune the guitar and breathe into it the tortured spirit of the blues which would possess the young guitarist whenever he touched the strings. Of course, there was a price to pay for such a gift and it was the traditional levy for supernatural talent – the musician's immortal soul.

One of the earliest and most enduring legends in rock's brief but turbulent history has it that Robert Johnson, itinerant King of the Delta blues singers, made a pact with the devil in precisely this fashion to acquire the spirit that inspired him to create the first articulate expressions of Western popular music.

Whatever the truth of the matter, it is a fact that in less than a year Johnson had miraculously transformed himself from an awkward youth with no obvious talent into a sharp-dressed master bluesman in full possession of his muse, or was it the other way round? Only nine months earlier he had begged local blues singer Son House to allow him to play a song between sets and was laughed off stage for his pains.

Johnson himself did nothing to dispel these rumours which dogged him to his early death at the age of 27 from allegedly drinking a jealous man's poisoned whisky. If anything, he encouraged and embellished the tale by penning such cornerstones of the rock repertoire as 'Me And The Devil', 'Hellhound On My Trail', 'Up Jumped The Devil' and 'Crossroads', which influenced a generation of bluesmen including his own contemporaries Howlin' Wolf and Muddy Waters, not to mention Elmore James who based his entire career on cutting variations of Johnson's song 'Dust My Broom'. These same songs later inspired the first rock guitar heroes, namely Eric Clapton, Jimi Hendrix, Keith Richards and Jimmy Page, who not only recorded Johnson's songs and stamped them as standards, but also borrowed the riffs to create their own songs which, in turn, became the inspiration for succeeding generations of guitar stars.

But it was not just the 29 songs that Johnson managed to record in the last year of his life that distinguished him from the other blues singers of the era – it was also his tragically short life and the manner of his passing that was to set the model for generations of equally tortured young souls who followed him down that lonely highway in search of fame.

The blues

Blues was not the only ingredient stirred into the intoxicating brew that was to be labelled rock and roll, but it was the most potent. A derivative of black American jazz, a blues is characterized by a rigid 12-bar pattern built around three chords (the tonic, subdominant and dominant) with minor intervals and flattened third and seventh notes in the scale (known as 'blue notes') to evoke a melancholy feel. Considering this rigid format, its greatest exponents (Howlin' Wolf, Muddy Waters and John Lee Hooker, to name but three) have consistently transcended these limitations to express every aspect of the human condition. Initially it evolved in the rural areas of the southern states as a form of worksong lamenting the hard times of the impoverished fieldhands, but when the migrating workers reached the big cities, particularly Chicago, they realized their acoustic guitars wouldn't carry their songs in the noisy bars. So they pawned their acoustic instruments for electric guitars, which had been a feature of jazz bands since the 1930s, and found that not only their music but their lifestyle changed with it. Instead of playing in the cotton fields or on their front porch for free, they were now finding paid gigs which gave them the wherewithal to dress 'sharp' and attract the women. Their music became harder, more rhythmic, and from then on they had good times as well as bad to draw upon for inspiration. The same style-conscious attitude and desire to set oneself apart from the crowd (not to mention the power to attract the opposite sex) have driven virtually every rock musician, male and female, from that day to this. Other popular forms of the post-war period to be distilled into rock included white country music, black gospel, crooner ballads, jazz, jump and R&B. These provided drums and bass guitar for the obligatory driving beat which was to distinguish rock from all other forms. They also supplied the instrument which would galvanize generations of youths throughout the world into selling their souls (or at least their youth) for rock and roll – the electric guitar.

All the way from Memphis

The creation of rock and roll on a sultry evening in July 1954 is traditionally credited to Sam Phillips, owner of the tiny Sun Records studio in Memphis, Tennessee, where B B King, Howlin' Wolf and Ike Turner had recorded their first blues. Turner and Phillips had what could be considered a 'dry run' for this apocalyptic event way back in 1951 when they recorded 'Rocket 88', a jump-blues with a boogie-woogie beat and a raucous saxophone solo by vocalist Jackie Brenston. It was a song which prefigured rock music's obsession with fast, gleaming automobiles, but Brenston was black, which forced Phillips to license the tapes to a black label, Chess, whose sales were acknowledged only in the specialist R&B chart.

The real catalyst, the midwife to this hollering, illegitimate offspring of white hillbilly and belligerent black R&B, which its creators were initially to christen rockabilly, was Memphis guitar picker Scotty Moore. It was Scotty who hustled Sam Phillips on numerous occasions to find the phone number of a promising 19-year-old white singer who had paid to record a couple of songs on an acetate disc for his mother's birthday the previous summer. Sam had suspected that the young truck driver might have the 'black' sound and feel that he was after and which he often boasted could make him a million dollars, although he hadn't got around to actually doing much about it.

It was Scotty who finally contacted and auditioned the gauche young kid whom he later described as being as 'green as a gourd'. And again, it was Scotty who recommended that Sam record him although nothing that the kid had sung had 'knocked him out'. Scotty's bass player, Bill Black, was the only other musician to be invited to the audition at the guitarist's house that sweltering

Sunday afternoon and he was none too impressed either. 'Well, it was all right, nothing out of the ordinary,' Bill recalled, although he conceded that 'the cat can sing'.

Enter Elvis (b.1935 d.1977)

So, when Elvis Presley, Scotty and bass player Bill Black strode through the doors of the tiny Sun Studio on 706 Union Avenue in the evening of Monday, 5 July 1954, there was no hint of what might be in store. Sam had booked an open session to give Elvis time to acclimatize himself to the studio and kick some songs around a little. There was no pressure to produce anything. It was essentially a rehearsal. Scotty had offered to bring the rest of his hillbilly band, the Starlite Wranglers, to back the boy up, but Sam insisted that guitar and bass would be adequate for what he had in mind. 'Just something for a little rhythm,' Sam had said. 'No use making a big deal about it.'

Nevertheless, the two-track mono tape recorder was rolling – just in case. The tapes could always be wiped later. But it was just as well they were recording.

After struggling through a couple of plaintive country ballads without finding that elusive 'feel' that they were seeking, they decided to take a break.

Nine months before, when Elvis was waiting to cut that acetate for his mother, Sam's receptionist had asked him what kind of singer he was, to which Elvis had shyly replied, 'I sing all kinds.' That was true enough. His taste extended from crooners Dean Martin and Eddie Fisher through jazz singer Billy Eckstine to the smooth soulful sound perfected by Clyde McPhatter. But when she asked him who he sounded like he candidly and truthfully responded by admitting, 'I don't sound like nobody.' Now that boast wouldn't count for anything if they couldn't capture the unique yearning quality in his voice with an equally distinctive sound that would make people sit up and take notice. Country music brought out his rustic, mom's-apple-pie southern boyish charm, gospel highlighted his soulful God-fearin' Baptist background, while R&B betrayed a barely suppressed sexuality smouldering beneath his apparently shy exterior. But on that scorching summer evening in July 1954 it was becoming evident that no single style could fully express the volatile cocktail of contradictions that was Elvis Aaron Presley. At least, no style that anyone could have put a name to.

While Bill and Scotty sipped on their Cokes and Sam tinkered with the equipment in the control room, Elvis, on an impulse, started strumming 'That's All Right, Mama', an obscure blues song by an equally obscure blues singer Arthur 'Big Boy' Crudup.

Elvis was only 'fooling around' as Scotty and Bill joined in, in the same off-hand manner, equally eager to let off a little steam before they returned to the serious business of recording. But whether they were aware of it or not at the time, something new was coming together, something spontaneous and joyful and as electrifying as a single voice and three instruments without drums could create. Something that could barely be contained.

Whatever it was it was carried along on a relentless driving rhythm that suggested a runaway train with the devil at the wheel. Scotty later summed up the appeal of the early Sun records by saying that they were 'a total rhythm thing – it didn't bother Sam if we missed a note, you just kept going and hung on'.

As the last chord died away Sam stuck his head around the open door of the control room and asked them what they were doing. 'We don't know,' Scotty admitted, somewhat embarrassed at being found out. 'Well, back up,' said Sam excitedly, 'try to find a place to start, and do it again.'

Rockabilly

What they created that evening and in subsequent sessions before Elvis left Sun for RCA in January 1956 had little to do with the quality of the song they recorded. 'That's All Right, Mama' was a straightforward 12-bar blues indistinguishable from a thousand other variations on the same theme. Crudup's version did not have the same intensity, nor touch the same raw nerve. Neither was it the combination of instruments. Innumerable country, jazz and blues outfits had performed with acoustic guitar, bass and electric guitar since the 1920s without creating anything like the same sound. Nor was it Elvis's voice alone, extraordinary and awesome though it was. But neither was it the distinctive sound that characterized all of the early Sun records and which musicians were still trying in vain to reproduce accurately on multimillion pound equipment 50 years later.

What was invoked that day by Elvis, Scotty and Bill was the restless spirit of adolescent angst which had been bottled up for so long that it simply could not be suppressed any longer. Before the birth of rock and roll teenagers did not have a voice. They were not even recognized as an identifiable group, but were deemed to exist in an aimless no-man's-land between childhood and adulthood. And yet, in the 1950s, with full-time employment and the end of wartime rationing they found themselves with money in their money in their pockets, but nothing to spend it on. They were also experiencing the emotional turmoil of puberty, but were expected to suffer in silence and contain their new-found feelings. Sex was a taboo topic. Black R&B 'race records' hinted at forbidden pleasures in euphemistic terms (rock and roll being a familiar euphemism for sex used in song titles as far back as the 1920s), but this music was also taboo to white teenagers. What the youth of the post-war period needed, although they did not know it, was a music and a culture that they could call their own.

If Elvis hadn't let the genie out of the bottle in 1954, Little Richard would certainly have done so the following year, and if not him then Chuck Berry or any one of a dozen young hustlers who were brewing up an intoxicating cocktail of styles in stills all across the southern United States during the pre-rock-and-roll period. Elvis was simply the first to make an impact, but the others were not far behind.

Ironically, its creators were as overwhelmed, mystified and exhilarated by this new sound as was everyone else who heard it once the first records were pressed up and distributed. 'We thought it was exciting,' enthused Scotty many years later, 'but what was it? It was just so completely different. But it just really flipped Sam – he felt it really had something. We just sort of shook our heads and said, " Well, that's fine, but, good God, they'll run us out of town!"'

Scotty wasn't kidding. For white boys to ape black music and sound as if they were enjoying it was considered by some little short of a lynching offence. Consequently, whenever Sam released an Elvis single he always hedged his bets by putting a country ballad on the flip side to appease the rednecks. But Sam needn't have worried. A local DJ played an acetate of 'That's All Right, Mama' and its flip 'Blue Moon Of Kentucky' continuously the moment he received it and from that evening on there was no turning back.

Elvis was the first teenage idol of the rock era, an archetypal symbol for girls to scream at and for boys to imitate. And he had all the elements that future rock icons would need – Grecian good looks, a certain reclusive mystique, oodles of sex appeal and, above all, youth. The ten sides which he cut for Sun and the dozens he cut for RCA before being conscripted into the US Army in 1958 define rock and roll. When demobbed the King, as he was then called, made a few sharply crafted pop singles, but was otherwise seen to have lost his edge and his hunger to surprise and excite his fans, his band and himself. But by then it didn't matter, others had claimed his crown and the music he had helped to create was rolling on a momentum all of its own. But it was Elvis who first shook them up.

Rock's impact

Of course, it wasn't long before the spirit which Elvis had unleashed was denounced by fundamentalist preachers, moral crusaders and outraged parents across the United States and beyond as the personification of the anti-Christ which had been conjured up to possess and defile the souls of innocent young white teenagers. According to these outraged citizens, rock and roll was 'jungle music', the roar of the Negro demon. They were genuinely terrified of what it portended.

Elvis, always charming, courteous and respectful by nature, repeatedly denied that he had intended to be provocative. Off stage Jerry Lee Lewis and Little Richard did likewise, playing the deferential southern boys to the hilt, but on stage they were the monsters of rock. Little Richard would reduce his piano to matchwood, then turn sweetly to the gaping mouths of the stagehands and say, 'That Little Richard, such a nice boy.'

The Sun 'stable'

In the autumn and winter of 1954/55 as Elvis's fame spread like wildfire across the States, fanned by electrifying appearances on national television, a queue of hungry young hopefuls made the pilgrimage to Memphis to audition for Sam Phillips. Among the first successful applicants were country singer-songwriters and future legends Johnny Cash and Charlie Rich, aspiring pop star Roy Orbison (who didn't find fame until the 1960s) and a host of genuine rockabilly rebels including Billy Lee Riley, Sonny Burgess and Ray Campi.

But from this impressive roster only country rockers Carl Perkins and Jerry Lee Lewis had a significant and lasting impact on the development of rock music.

Carl Perkins (b.1932 d.1998) earned his place in rock's Hall of Fame by writing the classic anthem 'Blue Suede Shoes' which Elvis covered far more successfully and with greater impact at RCA. Perkins wrote another half dozen rock-and-roll standards and played a mean guitar, but his voice was pure country and he was invalided out of the race for fame by a horrific car crash in 1956.

Jerry Lee Lewis ('The Ferriday Fireball') (b.1939) was a far more substantial figure who, legend has it, sold all the eggs on his father's Louisiana farm to pay for his trip to Memphis, where he camped out on Sam Phillips's doorstep until granted an audition. But his repertoire of blues, country and gospel standards didn't impress and he was sent away with the instruction to 'learn some rock and roll'. Three weeks later he was back, bristling with confidence and pumping his piano in a manic boogie-woogie style while hollering like a revivalist preacher.

With his first Sun singles, 'Whole Lotta Shakin' Goin' On' and 'Great Balls Of Fire' (both 1957) he put the fear of God into anyone over the age of 30, but at the same time he was himself a God-fearing country boy whose conscience continually berated him for playing 'the devil's music'. This contradiction invested his early records with a tension and an intensity which his teenage audience, in the emotional turmoil of adolescence, could relate to, but were unable to express themselves.

Lewis was the original 'wild man of rock', a flamboyant, swaggering, leering exhibitionist on stage who would provoke his fans to fever pitch by kicking back his piano stool, swinging the microphone stand round his head like a scythe and hammering the ivories with his heels. But his antics were abruptly halted in mid-1958 when it became known that he had married his 13-year-old cousin. In the furore that followed he was railroaded out of England on his first UK tour and subsequently denied big tours and television and radio exposure back home in the States. But 'the Killer', as he later became known, stubbornly refused to go quietly and bided his time playing a punishing schedule of one-night stands at fairgrounds and small clubs across the southern states until he clawed his way back in the late 1960s as a country artist. He is now revered as a cultural institution (although he would probably be horrified at being thought of in those terms).

The Sun sound

In the overcrowded and highly competitive music industry the sound of a record has often been as important as the song. A highly distinctive sound will distinguish one artist and his or her records from the glut of hopefuls who are all vying for the attention of the radio, television and press and, through them, the record buying public. The most successful groups and singers have almost without exception created their own unique sound and style, but it has often been down to the recording studio engineers and record producers to capture and enhance that unique personal quality with a distinctive sound that will be recognizable from the first crucial seconds of a record.

In the case of Sun records and other influential labels such as Motown, Stax and Chess, to name but a few, their artists shared not only the same stylistic traits but also the same studio and therefore the same readily identifiable ambience and atmosphere on all their records. Sun's trademark was a fast-repeat echo effect known as 'slapback', created by running the original recording signal through a second tape machine to give a split-second delay. It thickened the sound to give a greater dynamic to the smaller groups and it added much needed atmosphere (albeit artificial) to the driest of recordings.

It was a rough, primitive sound, limited in dynamic range by the quality of the equipment available at the time to a low-budget studio (a two-track mono machine), but it captured the equally raw, unsophisticated nature of the music that was being made. And most importantly, it captured it live, as it happened, with no over-dubs or technical tricks to paper over the cracks.

More rock giants

Little Richard (b.1932)

Little Richard, 'the Georgia Peach', was, in many ways, the black Jerry Lee Lewis. He was brash, outrageous, seduced by his own image and electrifying in performance. He looked like a black cherub in a baggy suit with a monstrous brilliantined quiff and pencil-thin moustache, and he was blessed with a foghorn voice that could penetrate the densest sound that his band could blast out. He was responsible for some of the most memorable and infectiously fun records of the era, including 'Tutti Frutti', 'Lucille', 'Good Golly Miss Molly' and 'Rip It Up', but, unlike Jerry Lee Lewis, Little Richard wrote most of his own songs. To anyone over 30 they must have sounded like utter gibberish, but from first note to last he delivered them with fiery conviction somewhere between a medicine-show salesman, a gospel preacher and a hysterical bordello queen.

And then, just as suddenly as he had stormed to centre stage he was gone, turning his back on rock to become a preacher. By way of explanation he claimed to have been saved from death in a burning airplane by the hand of God. To show his appreciation Richard threw his ostentatious collection of rings into the Hudson river, all $8,000 dollars worth, and strode into the first church he came to in Times Square, New York, taking up a vacant seat at the piano. Five years later he was back, just as uncompromising as ever and crackling with irrepressible energy, but by then rock and roll as he knew it was dead.

Chuck Berry (b.1926)

Rock and roll was an American phenomenon and specifically one which erupted from the southern states. It is therefore appropriate that rock and roll's most eloquent spokesman should hail from its heartland.

Chuck Berry, the first poet of rock, was born in California, but was raised in St Louis, Missouri. He has more claim that any of his contemporaries to be called the godfather of rock, having written more than a dozen 24-carat classics including 'Roll Over Beethoven', 'Sweet Little Sixteen' and 'Johnny B Goode' in which he summed up the hopes, frustrations and obsessions of a generation and simultaneously defined the archetypal riffing rock guitar style for future guitar heroes. His guitar solos are lessons in economy played short and sweet across two or three strings simultaneously to give them an edge lacking in the elegant labyrinthine solos of the jazz era, while his lyrics are wry, pointed observations on teenage life declaimed in a slick, slightly cynical, deadpan manner and emphasized with flashes of biting lead guitar.

Bo Diddley (b.1928)

Guitar stylist and singer-songwriter Bo Diddley was Chuck Berry's shadow, in the sense that both got their break while recording for the same label, Chess, in Chicago in 1955. But while Berry carved out a pop career, Bo stayed true to his R&B roots, which limited his popularity at the time but ensured that he became a seminal influence on the British R&B groups of the early 1960s. His early hits 'Who Do You Love?', 'Road Runner', 'I'm A Man' and the eponymous 'Bo Diddley' were built around his trademark rhythm (known as 'shave-and-a-haircut, six bits') and have all become standards of the roots rock repertoire.

Buddy Holly (b.1936 d.1959)

With his huge horned-rimmed glasses, puny frame and studious image, Texas-born Buddy Holly was the least likely looking rock star of the era, but in the three short years before his death at the age of 22 he extended the perimeters for future pop artists.

In addition to writing a clutch of classic songs in the country-rock vein ('That'll Be The Day', 'Rave On' and 'Peggy Sue') Holly was the first rock artist to co-produce his own records and the first to experiment with over-dubbing (recording vocals and instruments separately) and double-tracking (recording the same line twice to thicken the sound). He also pioneered the classic rock-group line-up comprising vocal, lead guitar, rhythm, bass and drums and he was the first to use strings on a rock record.

Ironically, his greatest chart successes were unfinished demo recordings which his co-producer Norman Petty over-dubbed with a rhythm section and orchestra and released after his death.

Eddie Cochran (b.1938 d.1960)

Cochran was another multi-talented pioneer; a sharp-witted songwriter, skilful guitarist, distinctive singer and accomplished producer, only he also looked every inch the part of the archetypal pop star. While Holly looked like the boy next door, Cochran hunched behind his huge semi-acoustic guitar like a cross between a young Elvis and the ill-fated teenage screen idol James Dean, an image which had a profound effect upon the next generation, including the young John Lennon.

Cochran's career was cut short in a fatal crash, but his attitude has endured and songs such as 'Summertime Blues', 'C'mon Everybody' and 'Somethin' Else' have continued to be covered by such diverse artists as The Rolling Stones, The Who, T Rex and the Sex Pistols.

Gene Vincent (b.1935 d.1971)

In contrast to Cochran, leather-clad rocker Gene Vincent was all image and little substance. He cut one undisputed classic of the era, 'Be-Bop-A-Lula', and a couple of worthy follow-ups, 'Race With The Devil' and 'Blue Jean Bop', but he lacked the songs to make a lasting impact. But rock being the ephemeral fireball that it is, that one true classic and his striking, tortured image as he limped across the stage wrapped around the microphone stand were all that was needed to ensure that his legend lives on.

Rock and roll music

The early rock records shared the stylistic constraints of the blues – a simple 12-bar structure relying on the three-chord trick (tonic, subdominant and dominant) in the major scale. In practice, this meant a song in the key of A major would begin with four bars of A major, then it would rise to a D major chord for two bars, go back to A major for two and then drop to E major for two bars before resolving back on A. This formula kept the melody within familiar boundaries, gave it an upbeat good-time feel and always resolved the song in a way that suggested completeness, unlike the rock of later decades which added minor chords and a myriad other subtleties to the maturing artist's vocabulary. In the beginning, rock and roll had only one aim – to get its listeners moving to the beat. With an accent on the first and third beat of each bar, rock was made for dancing.

As Chuck Berry declared, 'it's got a back beat you can't lose it, any old time you use it, it's gotta be rock and roll music, if you wanna dance with me,' which neatly summed up the music's appeal in the 1950s.

Again, as with the blues, rock's greatest exponents transcended the limitations of the format to create music that perfectly encapsulated the period in which it was made. Ironically, although it was created as ephemeral teen fodder with no thought for the future, it is this same attitude which has ensured that these records retain their appeal 50 years on.

Rock into pop

It may be a sweeping generalization, but there is an element of truth in the argument that in the mid-1950s rock was considered the sound of the South while pop was its fainter, less clamorous echo in the North. Rock was the rebel yell of the southern white trash (as they referred to themselves) and their repressed black neighbours, while pop was the polite and polished voice of the northern entertainment industry. Of course, in practice, the youth of America and the artists they idolized did not acknowledge or respect such boundaries, but as the categories of rock and pop became more clearly defined pop was seen as having a smoother, less desperate edge and a wider commercial appeal. It is a definition which still rings more or less true today.

One reason for the distinction was that all of the national radio and television stations as well as the major record companies had their headquarters in the northern cities and they were desperate not to offend their largely white audience. 'Race records' were segregated to the specialist stations and maverick independent labels, while country music (or hillbilly as they condescended to call it) was centred in Nashville and not considered exportable beyond the Mason–Dixon line. But as soon as Elvis started to have a string of national million-selling hits rock and roll was no longer considered to be a regional phenomenon, nor was it to be readily dismissed as a novelty dance craze which Bill Haley's success had suggested it might be. In response, the national media and the major record companies swiftly sought to control and exploit this new teenage fad, as they saw it, by grooming pale imitations of Elvis to appease the kids and clean up before the real thing swept them away.

And so before the majority of the nation's teenagers had the chance to hear the genuine article they were force-fed watered-down versions of Little Richard and Fats Domino tunes and a glut of mawkish ballads by white pop artists such as Pat Boone, Fabian and Frankie Avalon.

In spite of the entertainment industry's efforts to manipulate public taste, some white pop artists such as Dion DiMucci, the Everly Brothers and Neil Sedaka made a lasting impact because they didn't imitate, but were instead inspired to seek their own muse. Sedaka was a prolific songwriter with a penchant for penning cute teenage ballads ('Oh! Carol', 'Happy Birthday, Sweet Sixteen' and 'Breaking Up Is Hard To Do'), the Everlys chalked up 25 top 40 pop hits with their seamless close-harmony country pop, while Dion cut half a dozen timeless teen anthems (including 'Teenager In Love' and 'Runaround Sue') after honing his singing style on the street corners of the Bronx with doo-wop vocal quartet The Belmonts.

Rock and roll might have been able to dam the flood of manufactured music and ride out the storm of sustained assaults by the moral majority, had a series of disasters not stopped it in its tracks by 1960. That was the year in which fate finally managed to do what the media, major labels and moral majority had failed to do – rob rock of its creative spirit. It was the year in which Eddie Cochran was killed in a car crash and Elvis returned from the army, a shadow of his former self, to make a slew of mediocre Hollywood musicals and bland pop records. These events added to a catalogue of crippling disasters which had seen Little Richard denounce rock for religion, Jerry Lee Lewis run out of town for marrying his 13-year-old cousin, Chuck Berry jailed for two years on a morals charge, the hospitalization of Carl Perkins and the death of Buddy Holly. And on top of all that the music business was rocked by accusations of payola, the practice of paying DJs to play a record they probably would not otherwise have given airtime.

But rock and roll would be back within a few years, revitalized and reinvented for a new generation for whom Elvis and Jerry Lee would seem historical artefacts, but it would never be the same again. That, of course, was part of its charm.

Doo-wop

Fifties pop fell into three distinct categories. The first was composed of bland crooner-type ballads by the likes of Perry Como and Doris Day and inane novelty songs, such as 'How Much Is That Doggie In The Window?', which had been popular in the 1940s and were still enjoyed by young children and the undiscriminating. The second type was the new uptempo, strongly melodic offshoot of rock and roll as practised by Buddy Holly, the Everly Brothers and Neil Sedaka amongst others. And the third was doo-wop.

Doo-wop was in a category all by itself and is a form unique to the rock-and-roll era. It was an a cappella (i.e. unaccompanied) vocal style practised by young street-corner groups mainly in the Harlem, Brooklyn and Bronx districts of New York to attract girls, but also for the pure pleasure of making music without having to worry about instruments. They sang soulful, sentimental pop in close four-part harmony with a high tenor, a second tenor lead, a baritone and a bass; the lead melody being sung by the second tenor while the high tenor weaved in and out of it in a sweet obligato falsetto and the baritone and bass kept a steady wordless accompaniment from which 'doo-wop' derived its name. When they came to record, musicians were brought in to back them, but the magic was undiluted.

Many of the original doo-wop groups were black and their recordings were often 'covered' by bland white vocal groups who lacked the spirit and the quality of the originals.

CD collections tend to compile these vastly inferior versions, but the ones to look out for should include any of the following: The Monotones, The Five Satins, The Penguins, The Moonglows, The Flamingos, The Spaniels and The Cadillacs.

The appeal of the early records

It is the looseness and uninhibited energy which distinguishes the early rock records from the sanitized and self-consciously sophisticated popular songs of the first half of the twentieth century. Folk and country music, the only alternatives to the crooners which white teenagers would have been allowed access to in the mid-1950s, certainly weren't sophisticated, but neither did they have the combustible energy of youth. They were introspective and reflective forms which sought to preserve, if not actually fossilize, the cultural heritage of a nation, while rock erupted as a spontaneous reaction to institutionalized austerity and suffocating conventions. Although they didn't see themselves as such, rock's pioneers had no intention other than to kick down a few doors, blast away the cobwebs and loudly proclaim that youth was no longer to be seen and not heard. They didn't relate to the past, nor did they harbour any ambitions to establish a new regime to dominate the future (although that, ironically, is more or less what transpired). All that Elvis, Jerry Lee Lewis, Little Richard and the other early rockers wanted to do in the mid-1950s was break free and party – in the here and now. But first they had to find their voice.

The spirit of reckless uninhibited spontaneity which they unleashed has kept rock fresh, vital and restlessly creative ever since. And if an artist commits the unforgivable sin of growing smug, self-indulgent, contrived or complacent the next generation is sure to be right behind him or her bursting to 'give it a go and see what happens'. This is at the heart of rock's appeal. Its insatiable enthusiasm and its ability to reinvent itself and to express the preoccupations and obsessions of each succeeding generation ensures that it will always be relevant to the moment.

Soundbite: Little Richard 'Good Golly Miss Molly' (1958)

This recording perfectly exemplifies both the spirit and the structure of the music as well as demonstrating the ingenious way performers would overcome the limitations of the format.

The basic three-chord structure is disguised by having the notes of the chords distributed among the piano part (a technique known as 'voicing') rather than pounded out as block chords which would have made the song sound leaden and as simple as a nursery rhyme. The relentless onward movement is emphasized by a walking boogie-woogie bass sequence on the piano which Little Richard plays with his left hand while his right scatters the notes from the chords with wild abandon several octaves higher up. The bass guitar, rhythm guitar and a chorus of rasping saxophones keep the song 'grounded' by playing short figures around the root of the chord allowing Richard the freedom to go completely crazy at the top end.

To break it up further, to create dynamics and invest the perform-ance with a compulsive feeling of tension and release, all of the harmonic instruments drop out during the verses, except for stabs to emphasize the on-beat, leaving the drums and vocal to carry the song. A momentary silence at the end of each verse before the band launch into the chorus adds further to the tension.

Not only are the various instruments playing different parts of the same chords in a complementary fashion throughout the song, but they are doing so at different frequencies so that the saxophone, for example, does not block out the piano, etc., and the vocal and high piano fills can ride across the overall carpet of sound.

All of this would have been created intuitively as few of the musicians would have had any formal musical training, which makes it all the more remarkable. If they had been given any formal training in theory or composition they would undoubtedly have viewed the constraints of the three-chord, 12-bar format as something which couldn't possibly work!

Classic albums

Robert Johnson 'Delta Blues Legend' (1992)

Recorded over two session during 1936 and 1937, these stark, haunting songs of despair and self-doubt are delivered in a voice which hovers between cold self-assurance and an eerie fatalistic falsetto. Many are accompanied by a relentless chugging acoustic guitar anticipating the first wave of rhythm and blues by a decade and earning Johnson the title of founding father of R&B.

The raw primitivism of the 41 recordings (29 songs beefed up by the inclusion of alternate takes) obscures a subtle sophistication in Johnson's guitar style reminiscent of Louis Armstrong's sideman Lonnie Johnson and the jazz six-string specialists Scrapper Blackwell and Leroy Carr, suggesting that Johnson might have learnt his craft not at the crossroads after all, but from the phonograph.

Elvis Presley 'The Sun Sessions' (1987)

The Sun sessions capture the 19-year-old Elvis as he was in that seminal summer of 1954, untrained and untamed. His voice has a raw primeval power and a presence that belied his unimposing frame. One moment it is plaintive and appealing with a natural, indefinable beauty that evokes the spiritual aspiration of gospel; the next moment he emulates the wry resignation and sentimentality of downtrodden country folks, or suggests forbidden pleasures in the longing of a blues. Whichever quality he emphasizes, it's rarely contrived, utterly convincing and in some sublime moments chilling in its intensity.

Jerry Lee Lewis 'Great Balls Of Fire' (1989)

There is plenty of flash and fireworks on 'Great Balls Of Fire' and 'Whole Lotta Shakin' Goin' On', but what makes these 30 Sun sides indispensable is the obvious lack of artifice, the sheer animal passion with which 'the Killer' stamps every style of song he performs. Whether he is drawling a country ballad, belting out an earthy blues, making his peace with the Lord on a gospel tune or getting down with the devil, Jerry Lee holds nothing back. His piano-playing and singing style may be rudimentary and undisciplined, and subtlety gets short shrift, but the overall effect is exhilarating.

Chuck Berry 'Hail! Hail! Rock 'N' Roll' (1993)

Chuck's recordings are three-minute showcases for his songwriting and guitar-playing talents. The other musicians are subservient, blurred into soft focus in the background, leaving Chuck to spin his tales of teenage troubles to a steady back beat punctuated by his riffing guitar phrases and succinct solos. It is no exaggeration to say that the opening riff to 'Johnny B Goode' must have launched the careers of several dozen guitar heroes, all of whom would be proud to admit it.

These 28 tracks are lean lessons in economy, with no excess and no flash other than Chuck's stylistic flair.

Various Artists 'American Graffitti' Original Soundtrack (1973)

This indispensable soundtrack album is more than a collection of classic hits from the rock and roll era – it is a nostalgic re-creation of the atmosphere of small-town USA as the innocence of the 1950s gave way to the heady 1960s. Forty-one songs by such artists as Del Shannon, Chuck Berry, Fats Domino and the cream of the doo-wop groups are seamlessly sequed together by the voice of DJ Wolfman Jack whose presence lends an almost mythic quality to both the movie and the sountrack. Sheer magic. Even the inclusion of two cover versions by rock and roll revival act Flash Cadillac (who are featured performing in the film) cannot break the spell.

Ten essential roots of rock CDs

1 Elvis Presley 'The Sun Sessions'
2 Jerry Lee Lewis 'Great Balls Of Fire'
3 Robert Johnson 'Delta Blues Legend' (two CDs)
4 Little Richard 'His Greatest Recordings'
5 Various Artists 'The Sun Story Vol. Two Rockabilly Rhythm'

6 Various Artists 'Sh' Boom, Sh' Boom! 20 Classic Doo-Wop Tracks'

7 Chuck Berry 'Hail! Hail! Rock 'N' Roll'

8 Carl Perkins 'The Sun Years' (three CDs)

9 Buddy Holly 'From The Original Master Tapes'

10 Various Artists 'American Graffiti' (Original Soundtrack)

2 | SWEET SOUL MUSIC – THE 1960S PART 1

In 1967 black American soul singer Arthur Conley had his biggest hit with 'Sweet Soul Music', a tribute to the great soul singers of the 1960s whom he name-checked on each verse as if he was reciting a roll of honour.

'Do you like good music?' Conley asked in the opening bars, by which, of course, he meant soul, an exclusively black form of American dance music which had evolved at the end of the 1950s from the fusion of gospel with R&B.

Despite its name, soul was essentially sensual. Its singers may have been baptized in the fiery spirit of the Holy Roller Sanctified Churches which urged their congregations to lose their inhibitions, stand up, shout and praise the Lord, but on the dance floor their music moved their fervently devoted young fans in ways which were decidedly secular.

Soul singers didn't declare their affiliations in as loud and proud a fashion as did their religious brothers and sisters, and that is why their music appealed across the racial boundaries to both black and white. You didn't have to be a black teenager to be physically moved by the sinewy rhythms of soul, but in the early 1960s you certainly had to be a young black American to sing those songs – although, ironically, some of the steamiest soul records were made with white musicians.

Again, it boiled down to the fact that rock in all its derivatives was an American phenomenon. It is a frustrating fact, but a fact nonetheless, that before The Beatles broke through in 1963 only the Americans could make decent rock and pop music because only the Americans had soul.

Ray Charles (b.1932)

For some reason Ray Charles, the first of the great American soul singers, didn't get a mention in Conley's classic song, perhaps because he was never simply a soul singer. He was an all-round artist, a singer-songwriter, saxophonist, keyboard player and composer of eclectic tastes, a man with too restless a temperament to be confined to any readily identifiable category. Known affectionately as 'the Genius', he can be credited with bringing to R&B the elaborate vocal embellishments of gospel (known as melismata) which were to give soul one of its most distinctive elements.

Charles was blinded in an accident at the age of six and used braille to teach himself to compose. By the early 1950s he had his first hits and heard his songs covered by other artists including Elvis, who recorded 'I Got A Woman' in 1956. Charles's original recording of that song undoubtedly qualifies as the first real soul record because it has a sensual, syncopated rhythm and he soars across it as the mood takes him, while Elvis's version was pure rockabilly because he anchored it to a regular heavily accented beat and sang it as straight as a country bopper.

Although he was a seminal influence on successive generations of soul singers, Ray Charles refused to limit himself to one particular style. His biggest selling records were the gospel-tinged rock-and-roll songs 'What'd I Say' and 'Hit The Road Jack', but he also lent a soulful swing to pop standards such as Hoagy Carmichael's 'Georgia On My Mind' and a series of fine jazz and country albums.

Sam Cooke (b.1931 d.1964)

Cooke was a superlative gospel singer with a warm, mellifluous tone who found fame as a pop singer in the late 1950s with a number of self-penned romantic ballads sung in a soulful vocal style. Although his most popular songs ('Wonderful World', 'You Send Me' and 'Only Sixteen') are pure pop, his phrasing, intonation and plaintive, yearning quality have proven a profound influence on rock, pop and soul stars including Rod Stewart and Al Green.

James Brown (b.1933)

If Ray Charles and Sam Cooke can be credited with being the founding fathers of soul, then James Brown is surely justified in calling himself 'Soul Brother Number One'. In fact, with over 100 hit singles under his belt and more than 40 years on the road as a major attraction no one would dispute his right to be called the very personification of soul. Brown was raised in Georgia, the same state as Little Richard, and drew his inspiration from source as a member of a southern gospel quartet. The gospel influence is strongest on his early recordings where he rises from a hoarse, impassioned whisper to an anguished scream in the span of a single line. He kept the faith even after the hits started coming in the mid-1950s by incorporating the characteristic call-and-response format with himself in the role of lay preacher and his horn section urging him on to get on down and get funky, to use the idiom of the time. Clearly he was no longer preaching from the Good Book.

While his contemporaries were struggling to straddle the divide between gospel and R&B, Brown was laying the foundations for four decades of black pop by making a muscular rhythm the focus of a track rather than the melody. He could animate parts of a dancer's anatomy that the dancer didn't know had rhythm! From this point on, rhythm sections were freed from merely backing the singer to laying down a groove which would lock in and drive the song with the other instruments reserved for punctuation. And at the centre of this was the man himself, alternately seductive and defiant, mythologizing himself in the title of his songs, 'Say It Loud, I'm Black And I'm Proud', '(Call Me) Superbad' and the track which proved to be the prototype for the entire funk movement, '(Get Up I Feel Like Being A) Sex Machine'.

In the ten years between 1965 and 1975 Brown dominated dance music with an unbroken series of classic cuts including 'Papa's Got A Brand New Bag', 'I Got You (I Feel Good)', and the appropriately titled 'Cold Sweat'.

Thirty years after his first million-selling hit 'Please, Please, Please' (1956), he was cited as the single most important influence on disco music and 20 years after that he became one of the first artists to have his records sampled by young techno musicians who looked to him to provide the soul for their clinical machine-made dance music.

Anyone who doubts the depth of his influence into the 1990s only has to listen to Madonna, Public Enemy, Prince and any one of a host of hip-hop CDs to know that James Brown is more than simply the Godfather of Soul. He is a cultural institution.

Stax

If you need proof of the importance of a tight, turn-on-a-dime rhythm section look no further than the CD racks marked 'Stax'.

Stax was more than a record company – it was the soul factory operating out of a converted cinema on East McLemore Avenue, Memphis. Its official head was owner and soul fan Jim Stewart, but oiling gears and firing the furnace was the racially integrated in-house session band Booker T and the MGs (short for Memphis Group). The MGs played on every session together with a peerless brass section known as the Memphis Horns. Together they gave Stax artists such as Arthur Conley, Sam and Dave, Otis Redding and Eddie Floyd an instantly identifiable sound which promoted a type of brand loyalty among the fans who could be sure that everything on the familiar black-and-yellow label was prime dance music. Towards the end of the 1960s the MGs struck out on their own and had hits with light instrumentals 'Green Onions', 'Time Is Tight' and 'Soul Limbo' which later found a second life as television and radio theme tunes.

The label finally shut up shop in the mid-1970s, but its back catalogue continues to shore up the shelves of record stores around the world.

Otis Redding (b.1941 d.1967)

During his lifetime Otis ran a close second in popularity to James Brown among the soul fraternity, but he also became an unexpected icon for the hippies following his appearance at the Monterey Pop Festival a few months before his death in a plane crash.

His untimely death enshrined him as a legendary figure in rock's Hall of Fame, although almost all of his successful records had been limited to the specialist R&B chart with few making the crossover to pop until the posthumous million seller '(Sittin' On The) Dock Of The Bay' hit number one in early 1968.

His vocal range and depth of expression were impressive and meant that he could attempt a broad range of material from fatalistic ballads to grinding good-time stompers.

He left behind a small, but priceless legacy of immortal recordings which served as a blueprint for the Stax sound, including the self-penned 'Mr Pitiful', 'That's How Strong My Love Is' and 'Respect' (which was an even bigger hit when covered by Aretha Franklin).

Tamla Motown

Motown derived its name from its home base in Detroit ('the Motor City'). It was formed in 1960 by the 31-year-old songwriter and hustler Berry Gordy, who financed its first recordings from the royalties he had accrued from writing hits for Jackie Wilson and Barrett Strong. Gordy had been disgusted with the way Wilson's records had been over-dubbed with saccharine-sweet strings against his wishes and he was determined to be in full control of every aspect of the creative process from then on.

He was a shrewd businessman with an instinctive ear for genuine talent and he was almost obsessive in his desire to give his artists a polished, professional setting in which to shine. He hired the best songwriters, arrangers, record producers, engineers and musicians that he could find and kept them under contract so that they could create an instantly recognizable 'house sound'.

The artists were groomed, taught deportment and stagecraft and drilled in snappy, choreographed dance routines which meant that the less distinctive singers tended to become virtually interchangeable and, at worst, almost anonymous products of a hit-making factory.

But despite the strict regime and formula production process the label made some of the finest, most irresistible dance records of the era and established more than a dozen artists as household names, most notably Diana Ross and the Supremes, Smokey Robinson and the Miracles, The Four Tops, The Temptations, Marvin Gaye and 'Little' Stevie Wonder. Between 1961 and 1971, 110 top-ten hits rolled off the Motown line as efficiently and economically as the gleaming Cadillacs in the neighbouring car plants. Each record was stamped with the indelible Motown sound, which was slick and sophisticated with the vocals an integral element rather than a focus. The singers were almost secondary to the biggest beat on the block, with the lead vocalist and the backing singers often merging into one seamless voice and blurred into soft focus by lashings of reverb. It may have been a formula, but it was a successful one. Motown made party music *par excellence.*

The Golden Age of Motown came to an end when Gordy moved the company to Los Angeles in 1971, although he continued to rack up hits into the 1980s with The Jackson Five, Lionel Richie, The Commodores and Boyz II Men. The label was finally sold to an entertainment conglomerate in the early 1980s, but CD compilations keep its name in the charts.

Atlantic

The third of the big three 'soul stables' began as a small independent record label run by fans who also happened to be astute businessmen. Ahmet and Nesuhi Ertegun, the urbane and cultured sons of a Turkish Ambassador to the United States, founded Atlantic Records in 1947 to issue R&B records by Ray Charles, Joe Turner, LaVerne Baker and others, and swiftly became the leading R&B label in the 1950s. When R&B evolved into soul they embraced it with equal enthusiasm, signing artists of the calibre of Aretha Franklin and Wilson Pickett. A distribution deal with Stax led to other legendary names being added to the roster, such as Otis Redding, Solomon Burke and Percy Sledge.

But, as with their 'rivals' Stax and Motown, Atlantic were more than a label. Ahmet and Nesuhi acted as mentors to a host of great soul artists, encouraging them to develop their own personal vision and providing the facilities to help them capture these on tape.

Atlantic's other great asset was their technical team (comprised of producer and talent scout Jerry Wexler, arranger Jesse Stone and engineer Tom Dowd) who forged the clean, hard-hitting sound that became the label's trademark.

Wexler defined the label's appeal by saying that it didn't impose a preconceived sound or style on any of its artists, nor did it merely document the artists as it found them. Instead, the producer, arranger and engineer were encouraged by the Ertegun brothers to use their knowledge and love of the music to help the artists find their own unique voice.

Atlantic was sold to Warner Communications in 1968, becoming part of WEA. Nesuhi died in 1989.

Aretha Franklin (b.1942)

The woman they call the 'Queen of Soul' was not actually signed to Atlantic until 1967, the year when soul was entering its second phase as the politically aware voice of the Civil Rights movement. But her roots go right back to the source.

Aretha is the daughter of the celebrated gospel singer and Pentecostal pastor Rev. C L Franklin and she sang in her father's choir. She toured the gospel circuit while still a teenager and made her first records at the age of 14. But despite being hailed as a remarkable talent she failed to find the right label or material until she came to Atlantic, where Jerry Wexler and arranger Arif Mardin matched her impassioned but impeccably controlled voice with sparse, athletic arrangements.

By the time she left Atlantic in the mid-1970s she had recorded more million-selling singles than any other female artist and her shelves were straining under the weight of Grammy Award statuettes. Her 1960s soul recordings serve as a showcase for her four-octave range and soaring spirit, although her pure gospel albums carry a dignity and conviction that could redeem even the most unrepentant sinner.

Once you have heard the awesome Aretha in full flight, the contrived and shallow posturings of a Whitney Houston, Celine Dion, or Janet Jackson pale into insignificance.

Soundbite:
James Brown 'Papa's Got A Brand New Bag' (1965)

This is the single that established James Brown as the prime mover and shaker in the dance-hall and club culture of the mid-1960s and it remains the archetypal soul record of the era.

A brief anticipatory blast from the horns sets the stage for the entrance of Mr Soul himself, who ducks and weaves through the backline like a prizefighter in his prime declaiming in that gruff, gravel bucket voice of his the delights of getting down and getting funky. As Brown gets into his stride the rhythm section pulls away, flexing its muscles on a repetitive push-and-pull riff which is propelled by perky bass lines and staccato stabs from the horns. Brown had borrowed this idea from Latin music but he didn't elaborate on the basic line to the same extent so that the track remains sparse, lean and supple.

At key moments the characteristic 'chicken scratch' guitar of Jimmy Nolen chops in to emphasize the downbeat, but otherwise lays back so that the song's three-chord trick is cleverly disguised. All in all, this is a prime example of strength through simplicity.

Classic albums

Various Artists 'The Ultimate Soul Collection' (1998)

This is not strictly a classic album, but it is such a comprehensive collection of all the best sides issued by Atlantic, Stax and Motown during the 1960s that it has to be recommended as an essential addition to any serious CD collection.

If you are familiar with these timeless tracks only through 'Golden Oldies' shows on the radio, then you haven't really heard them as they should be heard in all their glory.

Digital remastering reveals that they were more than foot-tapping, finger popping dance songs with strong hooks. The wider dynamic range of digital reveals the detailed interplay of the instruments, and adds extra sparkle to the percussion, more bite to the brass, a gloss to the strings, a sheen to the vocals and a beefy, but rounded bottom end to bass and drums. No matter how familiar these songs might be they come up fresh and busting with irrepressible energy on CD. An indispensable compilation.

James Brown 'Live At The Apollo' (1963)

James Brown, self-styled 'Godfather of Soul', has always been a supreme entertainer and a barnstorming showman – the very embodiment of energy.

This set was recorded in 1963 at a time when live albums were extremely rare, but Brown knew that his studio recordings couldn't capture the raw excitement of his live shows and so he paid for this recording himself. It was a massive hit and has remained an essential album ever since.

These tracks prove that when you've got a tight band that's hot to trot and you're busting with talent, adrenaline and a voice like a buzz saw you don't need a big-budget video to stake your claim to star status. Slip it in the CD player, turn it up and get on your feet.

Otis Redding 'Otis Blue' (1966)

Redding's early albums have their share of highlights but are generally rather patchy. That leaves the three albums he made in the last couple of years of his life, 'Otis Blue', 'The Soul Album' and 'The Dictionary Of Soul', of which the first is the essential purchase.

'Otis Blue' is a consistently strong set featuring his compelling cover of The Rolling Stones' 'Satisfaction' and his original version of 'Respect', which in the light of the Civil Rights era assumes a wider resonance than Aretha's more personal interpretation.

If you prefer to have all the hits there are several compilations available of which 'The Definitive Collection' is probably the best and it also boasts a fair selection of indispensable album tracks.

Ten essential soul CDs

1 Ray Charles 'The Genius Of Ray Charles'
2 Sam Cooke 'The Man And His Music'
3 James Brown 'Live At The Apollo'
4 Otis Redding 'Otis Blue'
5 Various Artists 'Hitsville USA – The Motown Singles Collection'
6 Various Artists 'The Ultimate Soul Collection' (two CDs)
7 James Brown '20 All Time Greatest Hits'
8 Aretha Franklin 'The Atlantic Years'
9 Various Artists 'The Complete Stax/Volt Singles Vol. 1'
10 Smokey Robinson 'Anthology' (two CDs)

3 | THE BRITISH INVASION –
      THE 1960S PART 2

Prior to the arrival of The Beatles in 1964, and the stream of British beat groups which followed in their wake, American acts had resolutely resisted all attempts to break their monopoly on rock. Admittedly, they didn't have to try too hard. European imitators simply couldn't compete with the real thing. They didn't share the same roots, the same culture or even the same musical language. If Europeans wanted to make credible rock records that would be taken seriously Stateside, then they would have to create music that was uniquely theirs and not simply mimic the Americans.

During the 1950s records by Elvis, Little Richard and Chuck Berry were exported in very limited quantities to Europe where they were swiftly snapped up and prized by the cognoscenti, the hardcore fans who would accept no substitute. But the majority of record buyers were not so discriminating and happily accepted insipid versions of the original American hits that had been re-recorded by home-grown talent in lieu of the real thing. Every Western country had its Elvis imitators. France, for example, had Johnny Hallyday and Britain boasted the perennially popular Cliff Richard and a host of Elvis sound-a-likes with stage names contrived to whip up fan fever, such as Billy Fury and Marty Wilde. But none of these could hold a candle to the genuine article.

In these early days of pop the mass of the population didn't even know what they were missing, believing that popular music, as they would call it, began and ended with Frank Sinatra, Perry Como and the crooners. Beyond this they filed whatever remained into three convenient categories. Jazz was seen as a specialist taste for students and intellectuals, folk was viewed as something to be preserved but rarely listened to and classical music was for the genuine or would-be sophisticates. As for rock and roll, everyone over the age of 30 considered it a novelty dance craze that was to be ignored in the hope that it would go away.

Skiffle

Rock in the late 1950s was a teenage phenomenon and in Europe a generation of frustrated adolescents were burning with ambition to make music with the same spirit as the American records which they had heard on the Armed Forces radio, on juke boxes in coffee bars and clubs and on the soundtracks to the first rock-and-roll movies (see Chapter 12).

In desperation British teenagers turned to a home-made hybrid called skiffle, a term derived from a particular form of American folk-and-country blues which had been practised by poor folks in the 1920s. Lacking the money to buy electric guitars, amplifiers and drum kits, the British boys used cheap acoustic guitars, washboards and bass guitars which they made from a single string tied to a broomstick and stuck into an old tea chest. The music they made was as crude and rudimentary as their instruments, consisting of beefed-up British and American folk songs and a smattering of rock-and-roll titles performed with admirable enthusiasm but little effect. But it was a start and it gave some of them their first experience of performing before the public.

The Beatles (formed Liverpool 1957, disbanded 1970)

Paul McCartney and John Lennon began their songwriting partnership – the most prolific, creative and successful partnership in pop – in the unpromising setting of an amateur skiffle group. But they soon discovered that their shared admiration for Little Richard, Elvis, Buddy Holly and Gene Vincent could not be expressed without ample volume and a pounding drum beat. So they discarded their acoustic instruments and formed a rock group, or 'beat combo' to use the quaint idiom of the era, with friends George Harrison, Stuart Sutcliffe and Pete Best (soon to be replaced by Ringo Starr) and swiftly gained a reputation by playing local gigs in Liverpool.

It was Sutcliffe, a precociously talented artist, who supplied the new instruments through the sale of his paintings and it would be

Sutcliffe's German girlfriend Astrid Kircher who would create the 'Beatles look' which set fashion trends for the first half of the so-called 'Swinging Sixties'.

In 1960 the group decamped for the first of several gruelling residencies in the red-light district of Hamburg, where they were forced to play three sets every night to indifferent crowds of roughnecks and drunks. By the time they returned to Liverpool in June 1961 they were hardened professionals with a unique sound and a determination to make their mark.

They had also lost Sutcliffe in the process. He decided to stay behind in Germany with Astrid, leaving McCartney to take over on bass.

After famously failing an audition for Decca, because the company's talent spotter believed that guitar groups were on their way out, they signed to EMI in 1962 with whom they had the first of an unbroken string of 12 hit singles and nine albums (not including film soundtracks and compilations) and enjoyed success on a scale that was unprecedented for a pop act. Sadly, Stuart Sutcliffe didn't live to see his friends find fame. He died in Astrid's arms of a brain haemorrhage in 1962 aged 21.

In the eight years prior to their acrimonious and very public disbandment The Beatles became a musical and cultural phenomenon with sales only second to Elvis, and an impact on the popular consciousness which is immeasurable. With each new single they surpassed themselves, both commercially and creatively. At the height of 'Beatlemania' (1963–5) they regularly topped both the American and the British singles charts simultaneously, on one occasion knocking their own hit off the top spot. And with each new album they revealed a new facet to their writing, a depth of expression and a breadth of imagination which were truly astonishing. Time after time they surprised both themselves and their fans, which suggested a willingness to evolve using the creative process almost like a psychiatrist's couch.

But part of their appeal, part of the reason why they were able to fly so high was that they took themselves very lightly indeed. While 'serious' music critics were musing in the London *Times* and the American broadsheets about the complexities of their compositions and academics were studying their lyrics for subtexts on a par with the great poets, Lennon and McCartney were unimpressed and rather confused by all the fuss. They just kept knocking out classic songs with effortless ease despite the fact that neither could either read or write music. The contrast between Lennon's acerbic wit and McCartney's sweet sentiment made their collaboration compelling.

In retrospect their success was due to a unique and unpredictable combination of factors which have defied imitation. The group's greatest asset was obviously Lennon and McCartney's innate talent for writing deceptively simple but exceptionally memorable songs, an ability which didn't desert them until they went their separate ways in 1970. It appears that while they were together in the band their eagerness to outdo each other had created a highly productive rivalry.

Their songs became instant standards and were covered by other artists in every conceivable style, including symphonic versions. Their most widely covered song, 'Yesterday', is known to have been recorded by over 1,000 professional performers, a feat which contributed to the publishing rights to The Beatles' catalogue being valued at $600 million in 1995.

But their appeal went beyond the music and part of that can be attributed to their refreshing naturalness. Nothing was contrived to impress. Their songs, their image and their humour were as 'real' as their broad Liverpudlian accents. It was hard not to like them.

George Martin

But there was another crucial factor in their success, another ingredient contributing to the enduring appeal of their records – and that was producer and arranger George Martin. Martin was dubbed the 'Fifth Beatle', a title which gives an indication of the enormous extent of his contribution. With his classical training, technical knowledge, resourcefulness and encouragement The Beatles were able to develop and mature as musicians and as creative artists. When McCartney wanted to sing solo with a string quartet on 'Yesterday', for example, Martin didn't try to dissuade him but trusted his instinct and dutifully wrote an arrangement in keeping with the personality of the song. When the group wanted a harpsichord for the middle-eight break on 'In My Life' he hired one and played it for them. When they wanted a full 40-piece orchestra to improvise during 'A Day In The Life' it was Martin who found a solution amidst the chaos; and when Lennon couldn't decide between two contrasting takes of 'Strawberry Fields' (one with orchestral backing and one without) it was Martin who spliced the two together, having played tricks with the different tempos to create the illusion that one was a natural extension of the other. When they wanted to expand their soundscape as well as their minds in psychedelic experimentation on the albums 'Revolver' and 'Sgt Pepper' Martin gave form to their visions and helped keep their feet on the studio floor. And when they had tired of exploring and wanted to get back to basics he was there too for their swan song, 'Abbey Road', to reassure the world that underneath the long hair, beards, beads and kaftans they were still the supremely talented tunesmiths of more innocent times.

In collaborating with the group rather than compromising or cajoling them to get his own way, as many record producers of the period would have done, Martin helped The Beatles to redefine popular music and, perhaps most astonishing of all, persuade all of those people who previously considered that rock was only for teenagers that it was in fact the soundtrack to their lives too.

Merseybeat

In their desperation to repeat the success and impact of The Beatles, British record company executives signed up every group they could find in Liverpool during the 1963–4 'beat boom', but they predictably failed to recreate either the sound or lasting success of the 'Fab Four'. Some of the Liverpool groups, such as Gerry and the Pacemakers, The Searchers, Billy J Kramer and the Dakotas and The Swinging Blue Jeans, scored a few hit singles and enjoyed a brief spell as pop stars and friends of The Beatles, but none of these Merseybeat groups had a lasting impact on the evolution of pop.

After the talent scouts had scoured every inch of Merseyside they turned their attentions to other provincial cities in the British Isles. Of these Manchester proved the most productive hunting ground, producing Wayne Fontana and the Mindbenders, Freddie and the Dreamers and The Hollies. These finds were augmented by R&B

outfit The Animals from Newcastle and psych-pop band The Zombies from St Albans who, together with London beat merchants The Dave Clark Five and a crop of the capital's R&B revivalists, including The Rolling Stones, The Yardbirds, The Who and The Kinks, spearheaded the British invasion of America in the mid-1960s.

The Rolling Stones (formed London 1962)

If The Beatles were the tuneful voice of 1960s pop then The Rolling Stones were its sullen, shoulder-shrugging snarl. While the Fab Four aspired to have as wide as appeal as possible, the Stones contrived their image and antics to provoke parental outrage and attract the rebellious adolescents to whom The Beatles were seen as being squeaky clean. Ironically, both groups shared some of the same influences and obsessions, specifically Chuck Berry and Buddy Holly, but while The Beatles assimilated the influence of rock's past masters into their own, very British music, The Stones dedicated themselves to recreating the authentic sound of American rock and roll at its rawest, raunchiest best. Other British artists had tried to imitate the American originals, but those had been soulless carbon copies. The Stones, in contrast, triumphed because as fans they understood where the rockers and the bluesmen 'were coming from', to borrow the jargon, although their roots went no deeper south than Richmond, Surrey, where they had played their first gigs. The Stones didn't set foot in the sacred soil of the southern states until 1964 but, in spirit at least, they kept the faith. The Stones' early records were part homage to Chuck Berry and the (then) unsung heroes of black R&B, Howlin' Wolf and Muddy Waters, but once the songwriting partnership of Mick Jagger and Keith Richards found its momentum and its voice with '(I Can't Get No) Satisfaction' (1965) they were swiftly established as the cynical spokesmen for the 'Swinging Sixties'.

While Lennon and McCartney were turning out timeless tunes for mass consumption, declaring that 'love is all you need' and extending the boundaries of pop, Jagger and Richards were seducing the innocents with 'Let's Spend The Night Together' and re-establishing the ground rules just in case everyone went so 'far out' that they couldn't find their way home again. In the process they secured the sound for all the guitar groups to come.

As the decade progressed and pop's pretensions and the hippy dream dissolved into a turgid, lysergic nightmare The Stones appeared to be playing at its wake with the darkly decadent 'Beggar's Banquet' (1969) and the nihilistic 'Let It Bleed', the perfect antidote to 1960s optimism. With the 1970s the band appeared to be somewhat hung-over from the party the night before, although they managed to get themselves together to produce 'Sticky Fingers' (1971) and 'Exile On Main Street' (1972), two of their finest albums. In the 1980s they dabbled with disco and lost a great deal of credibility in the process, although they continued to be a huge live draw, so much so that by the 1990s they had assumed the status and earning power of a multinational corporation. But by then their music had mutated into little more than a media event and their records sold largely on their reputation.

But the group's impact went deeper than can be gleaned from record sales and stadium tour statistics. As the swaggering, pouting frontman of the self-styled 'Greatest Rock And Roll Band In The World' Jagger single-handedly created the role of the arrogant androgynous rock star, a persona which so many singers have since assumed for themselves. His attitude, mannerisms and barely intelligible singing style have been copied by artists as diverse as David Bowie, Axl Rose of Guns N' Roses and Liam Gallagher of Oasis. Guitarist Keith Richards has been equally influential, inspiring several generations of would-be guitar heroes to discard Bert Weedon's once obligatory *Play-in-a-Day* textbook and learn the rudiments of rock by copying his riffs instead.

Collectively The Stones roused a horde of 1960s 'garage' bands, 1970s punk pioneers and 1990s Brit-pop groups to haul some gear into a basement or garage, plug in and have a go. But they were also responsible for instigating the abomination known as stadium rock which turned a simple live performance into a spectacle, tours into a circus and records into a corporate product, the very antithesis of the rock ethic which had given the music its validity.

The Stones could also be accused of selling out to appease the establishment and of abandoning the barricades to become part of that establishment, but in the 1960s at least their music remained largely uncompromising. Add to that credit for a couple of dozen indisputable classic tracks and the impulse they gave to other artists and few could deny them the right to call themselves 'The Greatest Rock And Roll Band In The World'.

The Who (formed London 1964, disbanded 1983)

Legend has it that the climax to The Who's celebrated stage act was premiered one night at London's Marquee club when lead guitarist and songwriter Pete Townshend went into a rage after accidentally snapping the neck of his guitar on the club's low ceiling. Drummer Keith Moon, one of the original 'madmen of rock', thought he had wrecked it deliberately and joined in the mayhem with great glee by trashing his drumkit.

During the 1960s The Who's reputation for destruction and in-fighting tended to overshadow their music in the eyes of the press, music which would place them a close third to The Beatles and The Stones in terms of influence and historic importance.

While The Stones and The Beatles were charming high society and the British establishment with their pop-art pretensions, The Who had their noses pressed to the windows leering at the spectacle like grubby Dickensian street urchins. If they had been invited to the party they would have blasted both The Beatles and The Stones off their pedestals. The Who were not only belligerent, they were LOUD.

They began as a working-class band whose slogan 'Maximum R&B' and singles 'I Can't Explain', 'Anyway, Anyhow, Anywhere' and 'My Generation' won them a loyal following of young mods, but with the arrival of the hippies in 1966 the mods became an anachronism almost overnight. The Who responded by streamlining their sound and cranking up the volume to give any gentle, spaced-out flower children who were within earshot a rude awakening and one hell of a hangover.

But although the band wouldn't compromise or tone down their sledgehammer sound in tune with the times, by the end of the 1960s Townshend was feeling increasingly restricted by the three-minute single format and was aspiring to take rock into the halls of high art.

He found the ideal solution by writing the first successful full-length rock opera, *Tommy* (1969), where the broader canvas gave him more scope and a larger palette to bring his cartoon-like character sketches to life. He later admitted that it could be seen as pretentious and embarrassing, but that it produced some great songs, notably 'Pinball Wizard' and 'See Me, Feel Me' which penetrated the public consciousness to a degree that none of their previous hits had done, and it provided highlights for the group's stage set for years to come. 'Tommy', the album, earned The Who the unreserved admiration of rock fans and the respect of their peers while *Tommy* the movie, *Tommy* the musical and 'Tommy' the orchestral album brought their music to a wider general audience who wouldn't have let the band into their living rooms.

But its unprecedented success created its own problem which was that Townshend found it an impossible act to follow. His solution was simple; he didn't try to top it, but instead returned to his roots with the album 'Live At Leeds' (1970), whose monolithic slabs of sound provided the prototype for all the hard rock acts of the 1970s.

But the band whose most famous line was 'I hope I die before I get old' would not be allowed to age gracefully on endless revival tours. The Who effectively came to an end in 1978 with the death of Keith Moon, although they unwisely soldiered on with a replacement into the 1980s. The loss of Keith Moon suggested that none of the truly great bands would have had the same appeal if they had relied solely on the strength of their songs, the distinctive vocal style of their singer or the technical prowess of their lead guitarist. These groups became great because their music was the creation of a unique combination of talents, each of whom was integral to their distinctive sound.

The Kinks (formed London 1964)

The Kinks were just another carbon-copy R&B band until lead guitarist Dave Davies persuaded his brother Ray to join as singer, songwriter and rhythm guitarist. Through a succession of hit singles from 1964 to the end of the decade Ray swiftly established himself as one of the wittiest observers of the 'English' way of life. His keen-eyed character sketches were rather more downbeat and cynical than those of Lennon and McCartney as he contrasted the heady optimism of the period and its pastoral idyll with the routine reality of city and suburban life. Ray crystallized the laddish mod scene in the hard-riffing angst anthems 'You Really Got Me' and 'All Day And All Of The Night', then captured the fashion obsessives of Carnaby Street in 'Dedicated Follower Of Fashion', before summing up middle-class mundanity in 'Waterloo Sunset' and a host of other incomparable homages to the tea-and-toast culture.

Admittedly The Kinks had a limited musical vocabulary, but their quintessentially English songs captured the spirit of the 1960s more effectively and succinctly than many of their more accomplished contemporaries. In addition they unwittingly kick-started garage rock and later heavy rock with 'You Really Got Me' and provided the initial impetus, the basic repertoire and the template for both punk and Brit-pop.

Soundbite: The Beatles 'A Hard Day's Night' (1964)

The title track to The Beatles' first and, by far, their best film encapsulates all the elements which contributed to their initial success and what was then a radical new sound.

It opens with a G suspended 7th chord which creates a sense of anticipation and expectation, which is resolved only when the group crash in to accent every other beat of the bar. This is the 'no frills' approach to pop which is designed for a pure adrenaline rush. If you want subtlety the Beatles had that too, in spades, but this track was designed to whip up simple teen beat excitement.

This intensity finds release in the chorus with the line 'When I get home to you, I find the things that you do will make me feel all right', which has an echo of the double entendre beloved of the English music-hall comedians. It's almost as if the singer is sharing a knowing wink with the listener, although Lennon and McCartney were not a self-consciously clever pair. Their humour was spontaneous and artless, which is what made it all the more endearing.

Among the innovations which helped to distance 1960s pop from 1950s rock and give it a distinctive sound is the double-tracked lead vocal which serves to thicken the line, making it stand out more clearly, a necessity in this case where the layered guitars and splashing cymbals never let up or leave space for the vocal to breathe. Nor is there any attempt by Lennon, McCartney or Harrison to cultivate a mid-Atlantic accent, but rather the opposite. The Beatles exploited the uniqueness of their regional dialects as if to stamp the track 'Made in England'. And topping it all off are those characteristic close-harmony vocals.

Another interesting feature is the solo, which in the past would have been taken by a single instrument, but is here played by a guitar and harpsichord in harmony. Doubling lead instruments in this way has since become a production cliché, but at the time it signalled that this was not just another beat group.

The 33rpm revolution

Before the release of The Beatles' 'Rubber Soul' (1965) album, LPs were predominantly collections of singles padded out with a few cover versions of songs made popular by other artists and bolstered perhaps by a couple of original titles from the group's current stage set. They were often recorded live in the studio with the minimum of production polish – as was The Beatles' debut LP 'Please Please Me' – and rushed out to cash in on the success of a specific single. But with the arrival of the prolific Lennon and McCartney songwriting partnership the record industry saw how highly profitable a successful self-sustained group could be. They also began to recognize that groups could be seen as long-term investments and that their records might prove to be more than mere souvenirs.

From the mid-1960s the fans too had changed. They now expected their idols to earn their affection by proving that they were not merely performers but creative artists, writing most of their own material and conceiving albums as showcases for their talent.

At the height of 'Beatlemania' the typical pop fan was predominantly female and in the early teens, but when the Fab Four retired from live performance in 1966 and turned to serious creative recording the screaming died down and a new, more mature audience was established. The average age of this group was nearer 20 and they were likely to be young males in a secure job with money to spare for music which reflected their preoccupations, indulged their fantasies and fed their imagination.

The extended experimental song format of the psychedelic era (1966–8), the success of the first rock opera, *Tommy*, in 1969 and the advent of the concept LP at the turn of the decade reflected the taste of this new generation and helped to establish the album as the ideal format for serious pop artists to express themselves.

The dominance of the 33rpm 12-inch LP over the 45rpm 7-inch single was further reinforced by the increasing popularity of stereo LPs and the rising sales of affordable hi-fi equipment towards the end of the 1960s, which reflected the fact that pop music was evolving into something to be listened to rather than providing a steady beat for dancing.

Classic albums

The Beatles 'Revolver' (1966)

Sandwiched between the ingenious pop collage of 'Rubber Soul' (1965) and the psychedelic swirl of 'Sgt Pepper' (1967), 'Revolver' stands out as the most accomplished, faultlessly executed and fully realized of all The Beatles' albums.

It marks their emergence as serious creative artists rather than as simply consummate craftsmen. Every track explores a different facet of the group's personality and preoccupations in both sound and verse.

George Harrison's practical side vents his spleen against the Chancellor of the Exchequer's punitive short-term financial policies in the riff-driven 'Taxman', while his mystical alter ego emerges to pontificate on the meaning of life in 'Love You To' to the exotic accompaniment of a droning sitar.

Paul McCartney indulges his soft, sentimental side on 'Here, There And Everywhere', then redeems himself with the sharply observed 'Eleanor Rigby' before rousing the band to deliver the brash Tamla Motown inspired 'Got To Get You Into My Life'.

Lennon fares even better with three of his finest songs from this period, the languid 'I'm Only Sleeping', the truculent amphetamine anthem 'Dr Robert' and the mesmeric, mantra-like 'Tomorrow Never Knows' on which he encourages the listener to 'Turn off your mind, relax and float down stream' and later to 'surrender to the void'. From the man who had helped write 'I Wanna Hold Your Hand' only a few years earlier this was heady stuff.

And then, amidst all this hallucinatory humbug and soul-searching, Lennon and McCartney put their heads together to provide cuddly Ringo with a charming children's singalong song, 'Yellow Submarine', which had more than a few adults humming along too. No other group could have carried it all off so persuasively and with such charm. That was the essence of their appeal.

The Kinks 'Something Else' (1967)

The Kinks were the quintessential English group of the so-called 'swinging sixites', more so even than The Beatles, and 'Something Else' was the quintessential pop product of the period.

It boasts some of Ray Davies's finest songs, including the mock hero-worshipping 'David Watts' and bitter-sweet 'Waterloo Sunset', whose old-fashioned music-hall melodies and astute observations on the quirky English character make this album a unique portrait of mundane middle-class suburban life. Davies's ambivalent feelings give the tracks an undercurrent of cynicism and nostalgia which elevates them above mere pop, although that said, casual buyers might be served by one of the many Kinks compilations which will include all the familiar hits.

The Zombies 'Odyssey And Oracle' (1968)

Not all of rock's classic albums were recognized as such at the time of their release. 'Odyssey And Oracle' is still largely unknown by the general record buying public, but is cherished as a cult classic by collectors. It is one of the great 'lost' albums of the 1960s made by a band who were never really given their due.

The Zombies began as a British R&B outfit and were promptly signed by Decca who were looking for an answer to The Beatles, whom they had turned down the previous year. The group's first single, 'She's Not There', was a million seller in the States, but the record company failed to build on the interest and after making one album, 'Begin Here' (1965), The Zombies eventually faded from view. By 1967 they had moved to CBS, but were forced to finance the 'Odyssey And Oracle' sessions themselves using a mellotron because they couldn't afford an orchestra. However, it was a blessing in disguise as the ethereal sound of synthesized strings provided the perfect soft-focus backdrop for Rod Argent's lazy jazz-styled keyboard lines and Colin Blunstone's glassy smooth vocal. But the songs were too subtle for 1969 and personal problems were pulling the band apart. They split two weeks after finishing the record, but reformed two years later after its belated release. A single from the sessions, 'Time Of The Season', became their second million-seller, but within three months of it becoming a hit the group had split for the second and final time, leaving some of the classiest cuts in pop to find their own auidence.

Ten essential Sixties pop CDs

1 The Who 'The Who Collection' (two CDs)
2 The Beatles 'Revolver'
3 The Beatles 'Rubber Soul'
4 The Who 'Tommy'
5 The Rolling Stones 'Beggar's Banquet'

6 The Yardbirds 'Five Live Yardbirds'
7 The Kinks 'Something Else'
8 The Creation 'How Does It Feel To Feel'
9 The Pretty Things 'Singles 1967–71'
10 The Zombies 'Odyssey And Oracle'

4 THE TIMES THEY ARE A' CHANGING – AMERICAN POP AND PROTEST – THE 1960S PART 3

Phil Spector (b.1940)

One of the most influential figures in pop history was not a rock star, but a record producer, although he would be more accurately described as a sculptor in sound. Phil Spector (born on 25 December 1940 in New York City) was the *enfant terrible* of rock, a precociously talented and rather eccentric character who had been dubbed the 'Tycoon of Teen' to reflect the fact that he was a certified multimillionaire at the age of 21 from royalties earned on an unbroken string of self-penned smash-hit singles celebrating teenage romance. At a time when the pop industry was still in the grip of middle-aged executives, Spector demanded and received complete artistic control of the production process from songwriting through engineering to the final mix and rarely failed to strike pure gold. He was a shrewd operator who was highly selective with his releases, in contrast to the high-output conveyer-belt system which has always characterized the mainstream music industry.

Between 1961 and 1963 he painstakingly crafted dozens of perfect three-minute pop singles with a number of anonymous, interchangeable girl groups including The Ronettes (whose hits included 'Baby I Love You' and 'Be My Baby') and The Crystals (remembered for 'Da Doo Ron Ron', 'He's A Rebel' and 'Then He Kissed Me').

Spector's records were as intense and claustrophobic as the adolescent feelings they over-dramatized, each characterized by an almost operatic atmosphere which became known as the 'Wall Of Sound'. His innovation, one which continues to inspire producers to this day, was to realize that records didn't have to capture or simulate a live performance, but could be an impressionistic creation of the studio. He mixed his collage of sounds as a painter uses colours, producing records which sounded awesome on the tiny transistor radios which every teenager seemed to possess at the time. His secret was to cram up to 30 musicians into a tiny studio and have them double or even triple the parts normally played by one musician to produce a magnificent cacophony that seemed to burst out of the speakers like thunder. A typical session would feature four rhythm guitarists, a couple of bass players, three pianists, a drummer or two and a small regiment of percussionists who would lay down the rhythm track swamped in a wash of echo to give the illusion of space. By the time the vocals and a multitude of strings were added it sounded as if a whole orchestra and several rock groups had been recorded in an aircraft hangar.

If his early records were pop's Big Bang then his last grand gestures, The Righteous Brothers' 'You've Lost That Loving Feeling' (1965) and Ike and Tina Turner's 'River Deep Mountain High' (1966), were its apocalyptic climax, but they were a beautiful noise. Incredibly, the latter failed to chart in the United States and Spector retired with a bruised ego, allegedly becoming a paranoid recluse. In 1969 John Lennon persuaded him to emerge from the shadows to produce his 'Instant Karma' album and to put a gloss on the 'Let It Be' album which proved to be the coda to The Beatles' career.

It is one of the great paradoxes of pop that, having treated his own singers and musicians like puppets, Spector helped to redefine the roles of artist and producer so that from the mid-1960s singers and groups could feel confident of taking an active role in the creation of their own records and were no longer merely performers.

The Beach Boys (formed California 1961)

Between 1962 and 1966 Brian Wilson, resident genius behind The Beach Boys, wrote and produced 24 hit singles (three of them number ones) celebrating the all-American myth of an endless summer spent surfing the big waves, cruising Sunset Strip and chasing California girls. With songs such as 'Surfin' USA', 'I Get Around', 'Good Vibrations' and 'California Girls', The Beach Boys distilled every surfer's fantasy into three glorious minutes of pure innocent escapism, gilded by seamless, ethereal harmonies that were as dazzling as the sun glinting at the water's edge.

Ironically, Brian hated to surf. More remarkable perhaps was the fact that this astute and intuitively talented producer, renowned for some of the most blissful moments in pop, suffered deafness in one ear. Moreover, Brian looked like the boy most likely to have sand kicked in his face. He was said to be cripplingly self-conscious about his looks and disliked performing live – two factors which finally persuaded him to retire to his studio in 1965 in search of a more sophisticated sound that he could only hear in his head. It was the sound of the three-minute pop single as mini symphony with Brian and his brothers plus their cousin Mike Love and friend Al Jardine supplying vocal harmonies that would make every other vocal group sound like an amateur street-corner quartet.

The band's early albums had been essentially collections of hit singles with acceptable fillers, but Brian had tired of the sun-and-surf formula by 1965 and, inspired by Phil Spector, was looking to make each record a personal artistic statement. His answer was the stunning 'Pet Sounds' (1966), a sonically superior and increasingly complex set of tunes on the theme of passing innocence, which is said to have inspired The Beatles to conceive 'Sgt Pepper'. Although it was a largely intimate and introspective album in tone, typified by the aptly titled 'I Just Wasn't Made For These Times', it spawned two huge hit singles, 'God Only Knows' and 'Wouldn't It Be Nice'. These were not, however, enough to reassure the other members or their record company, who were becoming concerned about Brian's increasingly erratic behaviour, his artistic ambitions and his dependency on mind-expanding drugs.

The pressure to produce a follow-up to 'Pet Sounds' drove Brian to the point of nervous exhaustion and forced him to abandon the project, tentatively entitled 'Smile', before it could be fully realized. The problem was exacerbated by Capitol, the band's record label, who Brian accused of cynically undermining his efforts by issuing compilations of the earlier hits while 'Pet Sounds' was still selling. Fortunately, the release of the single 'Good Vibrations' (1966) left the critics inside and outside the band speechless and set the seal on The Beach Boys' unparalleled career. Though lasting barely three minutes this one sublime single had taken six solid months to record at a cost of $80,000 in studio fees, but it rewarded every painstaking moment by topping the charts on both sides of the Atlantic and it has since been hailed as one of the indisputable masterpieces of pop.

Perhaps it was not surprising that the band failed to reach the same heady heights again, although there were some strong singles and the odd album which rekindled the old magic. With the exception of The Beatles and Bob Dylan, Brian Wilson did more than any other musician of the era to redefine the role of the pop performer as creative artist. While The Beatles were content to collaborate with their producer George Martin, whom they entrusted with the overall sound of their records, Wilson had none of the Englishmen's restraint. Inspired by Phil Spector, he was determined to be entirely self-sufficient, self-contained and in full control of the creative process, which meant assuming the role of the record producer to ensure that his group produced the sound that he wanted to hear. He also happened to make some of the finest records of all time.

Garage rock

Punk was not a phenomenon of the mid-1970s, as is commonly believed, but the second wave in an assault upon the musical establishment which had launched its first attack in America in the mid-1960s.

The British invasion of the States, led by The Beatles, The Animals and The Rolling Stones, had inspired the formation of countless US 'beat groups' whose enthusiasm to imitate their heroes was often disproportionate to their talent. But in rock, youth and raw energy were often all that were required to create something irresistibly exciting.

These new groups were dubbed the 'garage bands' for the simple reason that most of them were limited to playing in their parents' garages because they were too young and inexperienced to get paid gigs. But even once they had persuaded sceptical club owners to let them take the stage they retained their casual amateur attitude and penchant for musical minimalism cranked out at a volume that had initially been intended to irritate the neighbours. The other endearing characteristics of a garage band included the reedy drone of a Vox or Farfisa portable organ, which sounded like it might have been taken from a schlock-horror movie soundtrack, and the presence of heavily distorted guitars which had been fed through what were known as fuzz-boxes. It was a raw, intimidating sound (especially if you were over 30) and often based around no more than three major chords because the band were simply too impatient to spend any more time extending their musical vocabulary.

Few of them played beyond their state line and fewer still managed to hustle record contracts. Those who did included The Sonics, ? And The Mysterions, The Seeds, The Shadows of Knight, Count Five and The Chocolate Watch Band – whose limited and fleeting success with one or two cheaply produced singles acted as an incentive to innumerable other young hopefuls – and the late 1960s proto-punks MC5 and The Stooges.

Others such as The Electric Prunes and The Thirteenth Floor Elevators anticipated the psychedelic sound.

Folk rock and the protest movement

Pop music had begun in the 1950s primarily as the inarticulate expression of teenage angst. But by the early 1960s a new generation of artists who had grown up listening to rock and roll were eager to explore the seemingly infinite opportunities that it offered for creative freedom and self-expression, when invested with integrity, intelligence and imagination. The innocence of this generation had been somewhat soured by the assassination of President John F Kennedy in November 1963, creating a disillusionment that was compounded by the increasing racial tensions in the United States, the cynicism of the Cold War and the fear of escalating American involvement in Vietnam. Consequently both artists and audience were no longer preoccupied with adolescent romance, but with contemporary events, while those with a social conscience saw pop as the most effective and direct medium for their political messages.

As the youth of the Western world became more aware of the world around it, principally through the influence of television and rock music, teenagers found themselves growing up fast and consequently rejected the contrived commercial sound of 1960s pop as exemplified by manufactured groups such as The Monkees. Teenagers were also becoming increasingly independent in their opinions and restless to find somebody to echo those beliefs. In America Brian Wilson of The Beach Boys and singer-songwriters such as Paul Simon, Joni Mitchell, Neil Young and Bob Dylan were eagerly adopted as spokespersons for their generation.

Bob Dylan (b.1941)

Bob Dylan (born Robert Zimmerman in Duluth, Minnesota) has been a profound influence on just about every songwriter to emerge since the 1960s. He was more than simply one of the greatest singer-songwriters of his generation whose lazy, weary drawl was admittedly a matter of personal taste – he was the man who gave pop a degree of self-respect and in so doing helped it to fulfil its potential as a true art form. It was not his fault, of course, that some of those who sought to emulate him took themselves far too seriously, affecting ambitions beyond their abilities and losing the plot in the process. Pop seems to have a capacity for self-destruction, to overstretch itself and take its musings as profound truths. Dylan was not free from these failings himself. He could be self-indulgent, occasionally pretentious and wilfully obscure, in a strained effort to create an enigmatic persona, but when he resisted the temptation to play the court jester he proved himself to be a superb wordsmith, conjuring much-analysed images with the playfulness of a poet and bringing a literary quality to some of the most incisive and perceptive songs of the decade. By the time he was in his mid-twenties he had penned more than a dozen songs which were to become milestones in the history of rock, and a couple of dozen more which would be classic songs by anybody's standards. Among these were 'Blowin' In The Wind', 'The Times They Are A' Changin'', 'Lay Lady Lay' and 'Like A Rolling Stone'.

Ironically, Dylan's idiosyncratic singing style and the rough-cut production values which characterized his own albums often meant that the most successful and popular versions of his songs were those recorded by other artists. The Byrds sustained their entire career on the strength of a handful of superior Dylan covers of which 'Mr Tambourine Man' is the best known. Brian Auger and Julie Driscoll scored a huge hit with 'This Wheel's On Fire' which Dylan would probably never have thought of releasing as a single, Bryan Ferry took 'A Hard Rain's A' Gonna Fall' into the charts ten years after it was written and, as recently as 1991, Guns N' Roses struck platinum with a cover of 'Knockin' On Heaven's Door'. It is telling that Dylan has admitted that he prefers Jimi Hendrix's version of 'All Along The Watchtower' to his own and later re-recorded the song in the style that Hendrix had made famous. Dylan had emerged in 1963 cast in the role of a post-war Woody Guthrie, the dustbowl troubadour, singing protest songs to the accompaniment of his acoustic guitar and harmonica, but he soon found the format constricting and the folk audience stiflingly conventional. Rejecting the role of their messiah, he appeared on stage at the 1965 Newport Folk Festival to ruffle 'the beards', as the folk fraternity were called, and in return was heckled, jeered and taunted with cries of 'Judas'.

From then on he felt free to make straight-ahead rock music and almost surreal lyrics, a mix which owed little to any particular tradition. This period produced two of his most accomplished albums, 'Bringing It All Back Home' (1965) and 'Highway 61 Revisited' (1966), before he was forced to take a sabbatical in 1966 due to injuries sustained in a motorcycle accident. Dylan returned to end the decade with a couple of country-rock outings, the intermittently inspired 'John Wesley Harding' and the patchy 'Nashville Skyline', before finding his form again on the aptly titled 'Blood On The Tracks'. This 1975 outing was a self-critical collection of songs which saw him picking over the pieces of his failed marriage with remarkable candour. It was followed by equally compelling 'Desire' (also 1975) which opened with 'Hurricane', a bitter attack on the American justice system and a plea for the release of a black boxer who Dylan believed had been wrongly convicted. But thereafter he lost his spirit, converted to Christianity and has been preaching to the faithful ever since. With the advent of dance music and high-tech pop in the 1980s Dylan's influence seemed fated to fade into history, but the revival of guitar bands and singer-songwriters in the 1990s has restored him to favour.

Before Dylan it could be said that pop was a mindless Frankenstein monster crudely stitched together from ill-fitting parts whose primary purpose was to give the kids a pleasurable thrill and frighten the life out of their parents. But after Dylan gave it a mind of its own it became a far more formidable creation.

Folk rock into psych-pop

Paul Kantner of Jefferson Airplane once famously remarked that if anyone claimed that they could remember the 1960s then they couldn't have been there, the inference being that those who were really involved were so stoned on acid (LSD) and other illegal substances that they could never hope to recall what it had really been like to live through that surreal decade. Now that the hash haze has cleared, it has become apparent that the band who were most responsible for ushering in the 'psychedelic Sixties' were not The Beatles, as is commonly believed, nor one of the experimental 'head' bands such as Pink Floyd, but a mild, unassuming Californian folk-rock outfit called The Byrds.

The Byrds (formed Los Angeles 1964, disbanded 1973)

These unlikely revolutionaries began as a coffee-house folk group under the guidance of singer-writer-guitarist Roger McGuinn, but swiftly added a rhythm section in response to hearing The Beatles. The band's choice of name was by way of tribute to the Fab Four although their sound owed more to Bob Dylan. This contrast between The Beatles' chirpy pop sensibilities and Dylan's world-weary cynicism created a hybrid that became known as folk-rock, exemplified in America by bands such as Buffalo Springfield, Simon and Garfunkel, Love and Jefferson Airplane and in Britain by Fairport Convention, the Strawbs and Steeleye Span.

Both The Beatles and Dylan were in turn inspired by The Byrds; The Beatles betraying the influence of both McGuinn and Dylan on their albums 'Rubber Soul' and 'Revolver', to the extent of acquiring a Rickenbacker guitar to recreate the characteristic Byrds guitar sound and aping Dylan's drawl on 'You've Got To Hide Your Love Away', while Dylan's decision to work with a rock band on 'Highway 61 Revisited' was prompted by the imaginative treatment his songs had received at the hands of McGuinn and Co.

The Byrds had taken off with a swirling, hypnotic cover of Dylan's 'Mr Tambourine Man' and featured no less than four Dylan songs on their debut LP of the same name (1965). They continued to fly straight and true with their second album, 'Turn Turn Turn' (1966), which featured two more Dylan songs and took its title from their second number one single, a radical reworking of Pete Seeger's biblical folk hymn, but there were equally strong originals in evidence which suggested that the band were maturing at a steady pace.

In 1966 to the horror of their largely teenage audience they jettisoned the jangling guitars and close-harmony vocals of folk-rock in mid-flight and took on board the exotic trappings of psychedelia. The first flowering of this beguiling bloom was the single 'Eight Miles High' which was ostensibly about the band's first flight to London, but was perceived as a description of a drug-induced 'trip' and was subsequently banned by radio stations on both sides of the Atlantic. The accompanying album 'Fifth Dimension' (1966) marked a clear progression in both songwriting skills and the band's sound, which were embellished with all manner of studio trickery.

This heady mix became even more cogent with the next LP, 'Younger Than Yesterday' (1967), a commemoration of that year's so-called 'Summer Of Love', where the guitars seemed to be imitating droning sitars to reflect McGuinn's intensifying interest in Eastern philosophy and mysticism. And yet even amongst the mantras they found time for yet another Dylan cover, 'My Back Pages', and the self-deprecating 'So You Want To Be A Rock 'N' Roll Star' which was covered in the cynical 1970s by punk poetess Patti Smith. The band's exploration of inner space reached its apotheosis with 'The Notorious Byrd Brothers' (1968), which suffused pop and sonic strangeness with the intoxicating scent of incense. But the trip had proven too much for founding members David Crosby and Gene Clark who left to rediscover their roots just as McGuinn drafted in singer-songwriter Gram Parsons to make what turned out to be the first country-rock LP, 'Sweetheart Of The Rodeo' (1968).

The Byrds disbanded in 1973.

Soundbite: The Byrds 'Eight Miles High' (1966)

In contrast to the chirpy pop of the early Beatles records and the strict tempo strumming of the folk fraternity this classic track periodically fragments into dissonance only to reassemble itself in time for the next verse. It is as if the band and the listener were sharing the same disorientating daydream and it suggests that for the first time in pop instrumental atmosphere is of equal importance to the vocals, which arrive almost as an afterthought. Until the vocals enter it is easy to imagine that the instruments could be left to convey all that needs to be said.

These opening bars are crammed with ideas as the track builds in intensity from a sparse, agitated bass figure baited by offbeats on the ride cymbal and a droning guitar line to the first key melodic phrase. This Eastern-style motif introduced by the lead guitar playing across two strings will return midway through the track to create the idea of a recurring theme and to reorientate those in danger of becoming spaced out.

As the drummer breaks into a tribal-like pattern on the tom toms the guitar line spirals into freefall, returning momentarily to lace the bass line with stinging streaks of distortion. And when the vocals finally tumble in (McGuinn, Crosby and Clarke in close harmony) with their travel-weary observations on being jet-lagged and lost in London, the drums appear to pick up the tempo only to play across the beat at the end of each line, thereby echoing the singers' feeling of disorientation. The guitar solo too is a world away from the once-customary variation on the melody, but instead echoes the dissonant explorations beloved by jazz giant John Coltrane. Nor is there a reassuring resolution to the track in keeping with pop tradition. Instead, the guitars drone into the fade like a nagging sore tooth. Few groups could make such a trip sound appealing, but The Byrds do.

'Eight Miles High' was among the first rumblings of 'acid rock', but unlike the bands who followed them The Byrds managed to say everything on the subject within three minutes.

Classic albums

Bob Dylan 'Highway 61 Revisited' (1965)

From the first chords of the opening track, 'Like A Rolling Stone', it is clear that the young earnest folk hero with the nasal whine and teenage anti-establishment rhetoric has matured into Bob the bard. In a speed-fed stream of consciousness which surges through the entire album we find Dylan mocking himself and the world that he finds too surreal to take seriously. The early influences are still in evidence; namely the vivid imagery of the beat poets, the restless spirit of Robert Johnson and the languid romanticism of Rimbaud, but these echoes are muted and always subservient to Dylan's personal vision which carries the conviction of a career politician.

With the able support of a fully-fledged rock band the one-time reluctant prophet and propagandist channels his passion into acidly amusing observations on small-town America ('Tombstone Blues'), youthful privilege and pretensions ('Like A Rolling Stone') and middle-class conventions ('Ballad Of A Thin Man'). The latter track contains the ultimate Dylan put down, 'Something is happening but you don't know what it is, do you, Mr Jones?', which summed up the polarization of the generations in 1960s America. But otherwise he is shrewd enough not to make direct references to the real world, instead recasting his characters as if they were extras in a Fellini film and giving snap shots of scenes that mix American myth, Biblical fable and Dadaesque dream imagery as in the descriptive 'Desolation Row'. Productionwise there are few embellishments to detract from Dylan's firmly focused vocal which carried the narrative flow. Some of the tracks are distinctly ragged around the edges, suggesting that the band had no more than a couple of obligatory run-throughs before the order was given to keep going whatever happened once the tape was turned on. But it is that element of risk which makes this album so vital.

Simon and Garfunkel 'Bridge Over Troubled Water' (1970)

In the post-punk world of hip-hop, Brit-pop and sampling it seems incredible that this gentle, introspective folk-rock album spent over six years in the UK album chart and was a regular contender for the 'All Time Greatest Album' award. At one time it seemed as if every home had its copy, and that wasn't far from the truth. Twelve million were shipped worldwide within the first few years of its release and it continues to sell decades after Art Garfunkel and Paul Simon went their separate ways.

The album's release in 1970 after a protracted gestation in the recording studio summed up both the soul-searching 1960s and the coming self-conscious songwriter cycle of the early 1970s. The format was essentially folk-based, overlaid with close-harmony pop vocals and a laidback 'soft rock' accompaniment which gave it a broader appeal than even the most popular rock acts enjoyed at that time.

Paul Simon's lilting, sharply observed songs explore the themes of fatalism, the search for fulfilment and the disintegration of relationships with an intelligence and a meticulous attention to detail that prompted some critics to predict that rock would soon become as literate and valid as any other art form. Art Garfunkel's contribution was confined to providing ethereal vocal harmonies, a subservient role that left him frustrated, but they were as integral an element of the duo's appeal as Simon's songs.

The anthemic title track with its orchestral pastel wash became an instant standard, 'Cecilia' and 'Keep The Customers Satisfied' charmed all but the heavy rock brigade, but perhaps the finest moments are the understated vignettes 'The Boxer' and the autobiographical 'The Only Living Boy In New York'. Some knocked it as sophisticated 'soft rock' for the thirtysomethings, but it is sheer class from first to last.

Ten essential pop and protest CDs

1 The Beach Boys 'Pet Sounds'
2 Fairport Convention 'Liege and Lief'
3 Leonard Cohen 'Songs Of Leonard Cohen'
4 The Byrds 'The Notorious Byrd Brothers'
5 Bob Dylan 'Highway 61 Revisited'
6 Simon and Garfunkel 'Bridge Over Troubled Water'

7 Joni Mitchell 'Ladies Of The Canyon'
8 Neil Young 'After The Goldrush'
9 Van Morrison 'Astral Weeks'
10 Phil Spector 'Back To Mono'

5 TURN ON, TUNE IN AND DROP OUT – THE PSYCHEDELIC SIXTIES

New fashions in pop and rock music have tended to originate in specific regions. Often a new sound can be traced back to a particular city or even a readily identifiable district. Rock and roll was brewed in the southern United States, for example, doo-wop in the Bronx district of New York, soul in Memphis (with a branch at Motown in Detroit), Merseybeat erupted in Liverpool and so on. The same is true of the music that dominated the latter half of the 1960s – psychedelia.

The San Francisco Sound

Had you been walking through the sun-soaked streets of Haight-Ashbury, the run-down bohemian district of San Francisco, in the spring of 1966 your senses would have been assailed by the pungent scent of incense and a kaleidoscopic collage of sounds throbbing from the garishly coloured stores and the Victorian houses which snake down to the Bay. None of these sounds would have been readily identifiable as 'psychedelic', for that was a term dreamt up the following year by the media and the record company marketing executives. By the time the 'men in suits' arrived in Frisco the original movement was already fading, middle-class American teenagers were naively latching on to 'flower power' as the next fad after The Monkees and bus loads of curious tourists were herded through Haight to gawp at the 'freaks'.

No, psych-pop and its blissed-out associate acid rock were not a single, readily identifiable sound, but a composite of diverse sounds and styles created by very different groups who came together spontaneously for one brief, glorious year-long summer to provide the soundtrack to a genuine youth movement.

At one extreme there were the folk-rockers on a day trip (The Byrds, Jefferson Airplane and Quicksilver Messenger Service), blues bands who had merely swapped their denims for kaftans and flares (Janis Joplin with Big Brother and the Holding Company), the eclectic and decidedly eccentric (Love, Captain Beefheart and Country Joe and The Fish) and even the odd-ball subversives from the avant-garde (which is being a little unfair to Frank Zappa and The Mothers of Invention, especially as Zappa condemned the use of drugs, parodied 'Sgt Pepper' with the cover of 'We're Only In It For The Money' and wrote the most cynical songs of the era, but he personified the heady surrealism of the period better than anyone else). Perhaps only The Grateful Dead, Jimi Hendrix and the UK's Pink Floyd qualified as being authentic psychedelic but they too diversified once the euphoria of 1966/67 had given way to disillusionment and cynicism at the end of the decade.

It was not so much a sound that they all shared but a way of life. The hippies saw themselves as the peace-loving 'flower children' of a new Golden Age, the Age of Aquarius, in which they would re-establish the Garden of Eden on earth free from the corrupting influence of mass, crass commercialism and the manipulative men in suits. In this naively idyllic new world everything would be free; free love, free food, free acid and, of course, free music. Drawn by the music and the promise of free drugs and free love, several million young Americans and several million more from other European countries converged on San Francisco in the summer of 1967 for huge tribal gatherings in Golden Gate Park that were dubbed the Human Be-ins. Across the free world young people rallied to the cause of Peace and Love as America intensified its bombing in Vietnam and racial tensions increased across the United States. They burned their draft cards, dropped out of college and turned their backs on comfortable homes to follow the pied piper and self-styled prophet of Peace, Dr Timothy Leary, who had urged them to 'Turn on, tune in and drop out'.

Turning on and tuning in was understood to mean 'dropping acid', loosening up and losing one's inhibitions, then 'freaking out' to bands who were equally stoned.

Psychedelia

Acid (LSD) was the magic drug that would set them all free and give them a new sense of perspective and new values so that they would never fall from grace again. LSD had, after all, induced the vision of this Eden in the first place and its insidious influence permeated every aspect of the new counter-culture just as Ecstasy would drive the acid-house trance-dance culture which swept the clubs in the 1990s.

The music that the Bay Area bands made and that, later, other groups around the world would make under the influence of LSD, was dubbed psychedelic, a clinical term that had been applied to describe the altered states of consciousness induced by the drug. Psychedelia aimed to recreate in sound the same sensory effects as a mind-expanding acid 'trip' and for that the groups needed to free themselves from the restricting three-minute pop format and what they saw as the mundane preoccupations of previous pop lyrics. As a result songs became longer, interminably longer if you were not 'stoned' or 'high' yourself. In fact, they were no longer songs as such, but streams of consciousness pouring forth from the inner mind, visions from a heightened imagination, or self-indulgent, pretentious, pseudo-mystical dirges depending on the quality of the acid available to both the artists and their audience.

Pink Floyd (formed London 1965)

The Floyd were one of the few groups outside of the States to wholeheartedly embrace psychedelia, but they did it in a way that was quintessentially British.

They professed little interest in the mystical musings of their American counterparts, preferring to draw on the fanciful tales of Victorian children's stories and the nonsense verse of Edward Lear and Lewis Carroll for their inspiration. Their first album, for example, 'Piper At The Gates Of Dawn' (1967) took its title from a chapter heading in Kenneth Grahame's *The Wind in the Willows*.

This approach was the idea of their resident eccentric genius Syd Barrett whose whimsical songs were in sharp contrast to the group's extended free-form freakouts which they reserved for live performances.

Barrett's strong melodic sense and offbeat lyrics brought the band hit singles, 'Arnold Layne' and 'See Emily Play' (both 1967), but his increasingly erratic behaviour due to excessive drug use and the pressures of success forced the group to ditch him in early 1968. He was replaced by guitar hero David Gilmour who took control of the songwriting chores and general direction of the Floyd in partnership with bass player Roger Waters. Together they steered the group into the realms of po-faced progessive rock with such monster-selling albums as 'Dark Side Of The Moon' (1973) and 'Wish You Were Here' (1975). However, there are still countless fans who annually mourn the departure of the precociously talented and infinitely more charming Syd.

Jimi Hendrix (b.1942 d.1970)

The dazzling displays of guitar virtuosity and the barrage of sound with which Hendrix frequently assaulted the senses were in marked contrast to his shy and sensitive nature. The enduring image of Jimi as a musical exhibitionist is largely unfounded. His habit of playing the guitar behind his head, between his legs or with his teeth was pure showmanship and served as a channel for the excess energy which might otherwise have melted the fretboard and blown out the amps.

His mastery of his instrument was total, the result of an almost obsessive dedication and the gift of singularly long fingers which enabled him to play a rhythm part with his thumb on the lower strings while simultaneously playing a blistering solo on the top strings. But it was not just extraordinary dexterity with which he astounded the public and his fellow performers. He popularized and perfected an idea that had been tentatively explored by Jimmy Page and Jeff Beck of The Yardbirds earlier in the decade, which envisaged the guitar as an instrument that could be orchestrated with feedback and manipulated to produce an entirely new range of sounds through creative use of effects pedals.

Jimi's albums were subdued in contrast to his stage performances, but they were brimming with new sounds and ideas. There were songs in the standard 12-bar format that betrayed his R&B roots, but transcended the format by his imaginative use of the previously untapped sonorities of the electric guitar. There were achingly tender ballads too, whose beguiling melody lines were ornamented with fluid leaf guitar licks. And then there were the heavy rock songs driven by short, repetitive riffs which were to give impetus to a whole new movement. In describing Jimi's music as 'heavy metal falling from the sky' one reviewer unwittingly named this new genre that was to change the course of popular music.

But Jimi was an artist who defies easy categorization. Having crystallized the essence of psychedelia and created heavy rock, his final recordings with the all-black Band of Gypsies suggest that he was moving into a more eclectic phase, one that Prince was to encapsulate two decades later.

On 18 September 1970 Jimi suffocated in his sleep from an overdose of sleeping pills, but his electrifying influence lives on in funk, rap, soul, blues, pop and rock.

The dark side of the dream

The Doors (formed Los Angeles 1965, disbanded 1973)

While the San Francisco bands were creating good vibrations and indulging in sonic explorations of inner space there were bands who professed a far more cynical and perhaps more realistic view of the world. The Doors had taken their name from novelist Aldous Huxley's drug classic *The Doors of Perception*, which had become required reading for the hippies, but the group's charismatic leader, Jim Morrison, was too tortured a personality to embrace the hippies' happy-ever-after philosophy.

Morrison was a film-school drop out with artistic pretensions and a predilection for obscure and morbid poetry. To all intents and purposes the band functioned as his alter ego and he led them on a different trip entirely, one in which they enticed their audience with bitter-sweet tunes and then forced them to face their worst fears and the darkest recesses of their own psyche. Listening to The Doors at their most nihilistic could be an intense and unsettling experience.

Morrison's all-consuming ambition to be recognized as a serious poet and at the same time be worshipped as a rock god by teenage girls produced half a dozen indispensable albums from 1967 to 1970 in sharply contrasting shades. There were quirky love songs ('Hello, I Love You'), grand guignol theatre pieces ('The End'), baroque pop ('Light My Fire') and rousing anti-establishment anthems ('Five To One') as well as covers of blues standards (John Lee Hooker's 'Crawling King Snake') and visits to the dark cabaret of Kurt Weill ('Alabama Song'). Morrison's self-destructive tendencies and avowed intent to indulge in Nietzsche's 'delicious ecstasy' inevitably contributed to his death at the age of 27 in July 1971, probably from a lethal cocktail of drink and drugs.

The Doors' influence extended into the 1980s, inspiring bands such as The Cult and Echo and the Bunnymen and found new impetus following the release of Oliver Stone's big budget biopic *The Doors* (1991) which starred Val Kilmer as the mythical Morrison.

The Velvet Underground (formed New York 1965, disbanded 1971)

The VU were one of a number of bands who enjoyed little success during their creative lifetime, but whose impact on rock was to prove enormous. They subscribed to the garage bands' minimalist credo, refusing to use three chords when one would do and applying volume, dissonance and distortion deliberately to convey violent emotion and alienation. Their songs were bleak in the extreme, which made them the archetypal proto-punks, but whereas the garage bands and the punks revelled in their ignorance, the VU had artistic pretensions. They knew exactly what they were doing, but they saw a virtue in a lack of sophistication.

Over the course of four albums they explored the seamier side of the American dream in a monochromatic soundscape that would not have been out of key as the soundtrack to a trashy porn movie. Most of the tracks were delivered in a deadpan voice by frontman Lou Reed, a singer-writer-lead guitarist with a sense of humour that was decidedly black. Reed's over-driven guitar always seemed to be on the verge of disintegration and one had the impression that the band too were operating on a knife edge, particularly on those tracks where Reed and the classically trained viola player John Cale droned interminably on one chord on the pretext that they were bringing the avant-garde into rock, but probably because they found it perversely provocative.

For a time the band functioned as an exotic pet project for pop art guru Andy Warhol, who persuaded them to recruit another protégé of his, the German singer Nico. Her heavily enunciated singing style added to the decadent cabaret atmosphere that they created on songs such as 'Femme Fatale' and the despairing 'All Tomorrow's Parties', but she left shortly after contributing to their eponymously titled first LP, no doubt despairing of Reed and Cale's endless atonal freakouts.

Warhol had provided the finance for the band to record their first album and also the banana logo that adorned its cover, but he didn't really understand what they stood for and, frankly, few people did at the time. Their songs, extolling the vicarious thrills of fetishistic sex ('Venus In Furs'), drug addiction ('Heroin' and 'Waiting For The Man') and transsexuality ('Sister Ray'), sounded a sour note in the Summer of Love, although they were to provide countless 1970s punk bands with the basis of a set list.

After the Velvets split in 1971 Lou carved out a successful solo career and was hailed as the 'Godfather of Punk', a dubious honour but one which was fitting. At one time Lou had summed up his personal pop philosophy by saying, 'One chord is fine. Two is pushing it. Three chords and you're into jazz.'

Soundbite: Jimi Hendrix 'Voodoo Chile (Slight Return)' (1968)

Hendrix had once declared that it was music that gave him a 'high', not drugs, and that his ultimate aim was to be at one with his music. With this track he surrenders totally to the all-consuming fire of his art in a virtuoso performance which has never been surpassed for sheer intensity and invention.

From a deceptively quiet introduction, which features the lead guitar line fed through a wah-wah pedal, the track crashes like thunder into a barrage of heavy chords. This riff, or repeated phrase, provides the onward momentum that fans of hard rock and heavy metal find addictive, but which the uninitiated might regard as mind-numbingly monotonous. However, in Hendrix's hands the riff is subservient to the flurry of notes he sends arcing after it. While the riff grinds on, careering down a hill like a juggernaut flattening all before it, Hendrix embellishes it with flourishes and fills that illuminate the supernatural scene that he is describing.

The format is a basic 12-bar blues although it is cleverly disguised by the polyrhythms and countermelodies flitting across the soundscape to give the impression of continual movement. The casual fills at the tail end of each vocal line speak volumes, but it is not merely the notes that he played which contribute to the effect, it is the three-dimensional sound that he wrings from the guitar, amp and effects pedals. By bending the strings at key moments he alters the pitch of the note by a semi-tone or more, giving a sense of suspension, of tension and release which is at the heart of blues guitar playing. A short tape delay thickens the sound of the guitar and echo adds space to give it the impact and dynamic range of a small jet engine. In combining manipulation of the strings with feedback from the amp and screaming distortion from an array of effects pedals Hendrix effectively deconstructs the tonal range of the instrument and rebuilds it before our very ears. It is no exaggeration to say that there are more imaginative ideas and energy in this one five-minute track than in dozens of heavy metal albums which sought to emulate its success.

And to close, Jimi invites us to continue sharing this almost mystical experience with him at a later date by singing 'If I don't meet you no more in this world, then I'll see you in the next one. Don't be late.' Heady stuff.

Classic albums

The Beatles 'Sgt Pepper's Lonely Hearts Club Band' (1967)

The Beatles transcended the genres that they helped to create, first with Merseybeat and then with psychedelia. With 'Sgt Pepper' they captured the optimistic spirit of the era, but exhibited few of its excesses. In contrast to the extended instrumental experimentation of the acid rock groups, The Beatles kept their flights of fancy grounded with wry working-class humour.

The jaunty title track raises the curtain on a typically English end-of-the-pier show whose varied 'turns' include Ringo's maudlin crooner ('With A Little Help From My Friends'), Lennon's carnival barker ('Being For The Benefit Of Mr Kite', complete with swirling fairground organ), McCartney in the guise of a sentimental Victorian music-hall balladeer ('She's Leaving Home') and Harrison as the exotic interlude languorously stroking his sitar and musing on the mystic East ('Within You, Without You').

The only truly psychedelic tracks are the dream-like 'Lucy In The Sky With Diamonds' (whose abbreviation to 'LSD' seemed highly significant at the time) and the dramatic climax 'A Day In The Life' whose psych element is limited to the discordant orchestral passages and Lennon's enticement to listeners to take a trip with the band as he sings 'I'd love to turn you on'. But in every other respect this was an album which realized the true meaning of the term, being a mind-expanding experience through the lucidity of its visions and the breadth of its imagination.

The only regret is that they did not see fit to include the archetypal psychedelic single 'Strawberry Fields Forever' and the equally influential 'I Am The Walrus' which had been recorded too late for inclusion.

Tyrannosaurus Rex 'Unicorn' (1969)

With its clutch of fanciful songs and intricate tapestry of sound the duo's quaintly titled third album evokes idyllic pastoral scenes inhabited by satyrs and fawns drawn from Greek mythology and the fantasy worlds of children's authors J R R Tolkien, C S Lewis and Kenneth Grahame. But even here, in this acoustic setting, amidst the leafy glades of Marc Bolan's fertile imagination, can be heard the faint echoes of Chuck Berry and Eddie Cochran. The tracks are a marvellous mix of fey folkiness, richly evocative word play and beguiling melodies delivered in Bolan's exaggerated vibrato, but underneath all the ornamentation and embellishments the songs are endearingly simple.

The 13th Floor Elevators 'All Time Highs' (1997)

Austin, Texas might seem an unlikely locale to produce archetypal acid rock, but between 1967 and 1969 Roky Erickson's southern psychedelic pioneers produced three classic albums which blended the primal energy of garage rock with the weirdness and intensity of the LSD experience. Their heavily distorted sound was characterized by staccato rhythms, eastern flavoured melody lines and an otherwordly wobble from an electric jug tuned according to the amount of marijuana stored inside it!

This compilation cherry picks 20 choice tracks from their three albums each of which was pervaded by the sickly sweet scent of incense, paranoia and a desperation to escape the ordinariness of the physical world into a spiritual dimension. This is music drawn from the very edge of sanity. Turn on, tune in and trip out.

Pink Floyd 'Piper At The Gates Of Dawn' (1967)

Psychedelia may have been an American creation, but the English groups eloquently expressed its more fanciful and imaginative aspects. With the eccentric Syd Barrett at the helm, The Floyd were in a better position than most to explore the inner landscapes of the mind and convey its surreal vistas with a child-like wonder. Barrett's fractured, offbeat guitar style and whimsical wordplay invests these tracks with a singular slant on the acid experience and a curious charm which has lost little of its appeal over the years. The two seminal singles of the Barrett period, 'See Emily Play' and 'Arnold Layne', are to be found elsewhere, but the group's first and only album with their founder contains ten essential psych-pop gems and a prototypical instrumental acid rock anthem, 'Interstellar Overdrive', which helped offset the band's later excesses.

Ten essential psych-pop CDs

1 The Beatles 'Sgt Pepper's Lonely Hearts Club Band'
2 Tyrannosaurus Rex 'Unicorn'
3 The Velvet Underground 'The Velvet Underground And Nico'
4 The Doors 'The Doors'
5 Jimi Hendrix 'The Ultimate Experience'
6 The 13th Floor Elevators 'All Time Highs'
7 Various Artists 'Nuggets – Original Artyfacts From The First Psychedelic Era 1965–68'
8 Love 'Da Capo'
9 Pink Floyd 'Piper At The Gates Of Dawn'
10 Country Joe and The Fish 'Electric Music For The Mind And Body'

6 | STADIUMS AND SUPERGROUPS – LATE 1960S AND EARLY 1970S

The inevitable consequence of the 'beat boom' and blues revival in the mid-1960s was that bands on both sides of the Atlantic began to explore the possibilities beyond the three-chord 12-bar format once they found that they could write original material. Many retained the riff-driven, back-to-basics approach, but tricked up their own songs with demonstrative vocal and guitar histrionics which had been one side effect of the psychedelic experience. Of these bands Cream, Led Zeppelin, Deep Purple and Black Sabbath made a lasting and profound impression on the development of popular music and racked up several multimillion-selling albums in the process.

A second stream shook off what they saw as the restrictions imposed by the blues and evolved an entirely new and experimental form rooted in rock, but aimed squarely into the future. These 'progressive' rock bands strove to blur the boundaries between rock and classical music, a laudable enough ambition and one which they achieved with varying degrees of success. Of these groups King Crimson, ELP, Yes, Genesis, The Moody Blues and Jethro Tull were the most successful although, ironically, it is their sound and vision that has dated more dramatically than their less ambitious contemporaries. One reason for this is that the progressive groups augmented their sound with keyboards, specifically the then fashionable Moog synthesizer and the notoriously unreliable mellotron, which provided the ethereal string sounds triggered by tiny tape loops. Guitars, drums and bass alone simply couldn't evoke the atmosphere, nor provide the broad spectrum of additional colours that these (mostly classically trained) musicians required, but in comparison with the pure digitally sampled sounds of the 1990s some of the keyboards used in the 1960s and 1970s were positively primitive and wholly unrealistic.

So, what we witnessed in the late 1960s and early 1970s was a splintering of popular music into several distinctly different and incompatible camps. In one the hard rock and heavy metal outfits eschewed a belief in what was once dubbed 'heads-down-no-nonsense-mindless-boogie' with a guitar star indulging in endless extended solos on the pretext of self-expression, but more often than not simply because he couldn't resist showing off. In the other camp the prog-rock or pomp-rock contingent would turn the spotlight on the keyboard player to similar effect. However, whichever camp you gravitated towards there was always the threat that for live performances, and even on record, the band might have lost all sense of proportion and also allowed their drummer a 20-minute solo!

It's easy to be cynical about rock in the early 1970s, because it seemed to have lost its simplicity and sense of humour. The initial innocence and enthusiasm of the pre-psychedelic period appeared to have been replaced by a straight-faced, overserious, almost religious fervour in which singers became political pundits or spiritual gurus; drummers, bass players and keyboard players were hailed as virtuosi; and guitarists were no longer merely musicians but guitar heroes, or in the case of Eric Clapton known commonly as 'God'.

Eric Clapton (b.1945)

Eric Clapton is the epitome of that old music-biz cliché the 'musician's musician'. Shy, soft spoken and self-effacing, he has always shunned publicity, preferring to express himself through the eloquence of his guitar. In The Yardbirds, and briefly with John Mayall's Bluesbreakers, he worked out the guilt, anger and sadness of an unhappy childhood (his parents abandoned him and he was brought up by foster parents) to emerge as possibly the finest white blues guitarist of them all.

Clapton began his recording career with R&B revivalists The Yardbirds shortly after their formation in 1963. However, the band soon abandoned their purest roots in favour of psychedelic pop, alienating both their earlier audience and Clapton, who left in March 1965 to be replaced by future legends Jimmy Page and Jeff Beck.

Clapton then joined John Mayall, a man who was seen as the

godfather of the British blues movement and whose band The Bluesbreakers acted as a finishing school for many aspiring musicians who then went on to greater things. The Mayall material demonstrates both Clapton's remarkable technique and his depth of feeling for traditional and original blues while offering the opportunity for blistering solos on the verge of feedback – a foretaste of things to come.

With Cream, the first of the 'supergroups' (formed by musicians who had established formidable reputations in previous bands), he displayed all the ebullience of youth, crossing egos with bassist Jack Bruce and drummer Ginger Baker, until technique took precedence over everything else and they split, leaving Clapton intimidated by his own reputation.

During a brief spell in the ill-fated Blind Faith he found reassurance in religion and conveyed that faith in the emotive and uplifting 'Presence Of The Lord'. Then when his girlfriend Patti Boyd left him to return to her husband, ex-Beatle George Harrison, he poured out his angst in the classic anthem 'Layla', a track which features one of the most famous guitar riffs in rock. The accompanying album, 'Layla And Other Assorted Love Songs', was one of the great 'buddy' albums of the era on which he traded licks with American Duane Allman on the understated 'Bell Bottom Blues', the plaintive 'Nobody Knows You When You're Down And Out' and the fatalistic 'Key To The Highway'. Eric had chosen to hide behind the anonymity of the band name Derek and the Dominoes, evidently in need of a break after having had every solo scrutinized during his stint with Cream. The album, a double, was a relative failure on release. Critics and public alike – who expected long tortured solos – were disappointed by Eric's economical and easy-going style and the single version of 'Layla' was only acknowledged as a classic on re-release.

He then settled down to make the first in a series of largely uninspired country flavoured solo albums which satisfied the mainstream market but disappointed his old fans. His first solo LP 'Eric Clapton' included his first American hit, a cover of J J Cale's 'After Midnight', which set the style for all his subsequent solo outings. Gone were the fretboard fireworks of his youth and in their place short fluid licks which complemented his equally understated vocals.

Following a successful battle with heroin in the early 1970s, the man they called 'Slowhand' returned to the recording studio in mellower mood, establishing himself as a steady hit maker with the album '461 Ocean Boulevard' (1974) and single 'I Shot The Sheriff'. Only with the two Phil Collins-produced albums 'Behind the Sun' (1985) and 'August' (1986) and the back-to-the-roots blues project 'From The Cradle' (1994) was some of the old fire rekindled.

Time and again Clapton has confounded his critics, who saw him as a relic from the 1960s, proving himself to be not only a consummate musician but living proof that you don't have to be black or American to play the blues. Although he appears to have forsaken the flamboyant guitar heroics of his youth he remains Britain's most versatile guitar hero.

Cream (formed 1966, disbanded 1968)

By the time Clapton left Mayall in mid-1966 the legend 'Clapton is God' was to be seen sprayed on innumerable walls the length and breadth of Britain. Clapton's reputation had dwarfed that of his mentor who encouraged the young guitarist to form his own band with ex-Graham Bond men Jack Bruce and Ginger Baker.

Bruce was a fluid bass player with a leaning towards jazz who sought to raise the bass from its secondary status to that of a lead instrument. Baker was a flamboyant but powerful percussionist who shared Bruce and Clapton's frustration with the limitations of the three-minute single. Together they sought to expand the boundaries of rock through extended improvisations based on the blues. Widely acknowledged as individual virtuosi, the trio promptly named themselves Cream and cut their first album, 'Fresh Cream', in 1966. It was a somewhat disappointing debut, an uneasy blend of straight mid-1960s pop ('I Feel Free', 'Dreaming', 'Wrapping Paper', 'The Coffee Song') and blues, both original ('Sleepy Time Time') and traditional ('Spoonful', 'Rollin' And Tumblin'', 'Cat's Squirrel', 'I'm So Glad'). The traditional tracks still sound exciting, but it wasn't until they were reworked outside the restrictions of the recording studio (for the live sides of 'Wheels Of Fire' and the superb 'Live Cream Volume One') that their true potential was realized. Cream were essentially a live band who regarded songs merely as a basis for improvisation.

Nevertheless, they did come up with a handful of classic originals, three of which were included on their second LP 'Disraeli Gears' in 1967. 'Sunshine Of Your Love', 'Tales Of Brave Ulysses' and 'Strange Brew' (based on the blues original 'Lawdy Mama') featured some of Clapton's most lyrical and expressive guitar work and set the standard for generations of heavy rock acts.

'Wheels Of Fire' (1968), a double album featuring a studio set and two live sides, is an essential purchase if only for Clapton's 15-minute solo on 'Spoonful' and his superlative version of Robert Johnson's 'Crossroads'. It would be charitable to see Baker's 16-minute drum solo, 'Toad', as an artefact of the era.

The studio sides were more consistent, boasting the belligerent blues 'Born Under A Bad Sign' and 'Politician' plus the supreme 'White Room' which proved that given the right material Cream were potentially the intimate power rock trio of the 1960s. Unfortunately, their choice of material did not always match the quality of their musicianship, and what should have been their definitive offering is instead indicative of both the band's lack of focus and the times which spawned them.

Clapton was the first to realize it had all got out of hand. During their last American tour he allegedly stopped playing just to see if the others noticed. They didn't, and soon after the first supergroup was disbanded. A typically patchy posthumous LP 'Goodbye Cream' was released in 1968 featuring excellent live versions of 'I'm So Glad', 'Politician' and 'Sitting On Top Of The World' and four studio tracks, of which 'Badge', written by Clapton and George Harrison, is the most enduring. It was a fitting if flawed epitaph to a group and an ideology that could only have flowered in the 1960s.

Led Zeppelin (formed 1969, disbanded 1980)

To label Led Zeppelin 'heavy rock' and file them with the host of derivative heavy metal merchants who cruised on one memorable riff for most of their careers is to do the group a great disservice. Zeppelin, like Cream before them, had a broad range of influences from which they drew inspiration. Combining the raw intensity of the blues with the delicate introspection of folk, Zeppelin produced nine multimillion-selling albums of considerable variety between 1969 and their demise in 1980.

The Led Zeppelin story began in 1968 when ex-Yardbirds guitarist Jimmy Page and seasoned session bass player John Paul Jones persuaded Roger Plant and drummer John Bonham to form a band to fulfil The Yardbirds' outstanding touring commitments. Plant provided the impassioned vocals in an eerie falsetto that recalls the great blues singers of the past; Page demonstrated an almost paranormal power over the guitar from which he coaxed a voice as ardent and eloquent as any singer; while John Paul Jones ornamented some of their tracks with sparse keyboard fills but otherwise settled for laying a solid foundation with the ever-dependable Bonham.

Their debut album (see 'Classic albums' below) was essentially a heavy blues set whose rigid, traditional 12-bar structures were softened at the edges by Plant's soulful vocals, John Paul Jones' loose flowing bass lines, Jimmy Page's lyrical lead guitar licks and John Bonham's sprawling drum fills.

Their second album marked a development into sparse, smouldering, riff-driven rock contrasted against beefed-up acoustic tunes with fashionably Tolkienesque themes. The music on this second outing (title simply 'Led Zeppelin II') was more muscular as opposed to its lean-sounding predecessor and the lead guitar had become as much a feature as the vocals.

The focus softened for the third album (predictably titled 'Led Zeppelin III') which had a distinct folk-rock flavour with only the occasional blues interlude and the uncharacteristically belligerent opener 'The Immigrant Song', a relentless pounding paean to the Norse gods and the pleasures awaiting their faithful warriors in Valhalla. The otherwise subdued set disappointed the dedicated heavy rock brigade who wanted wall-to-wall riffing, but the band were clearly intent on demonstrating their versatility.

The release of their (again untitled) fourth album pleased all factions with its more evenly balanced mix of hard rock and folky acoustic numbers and by the inclusion of the track which magically managed to combine all the elements in one majestic eight-minute opus, 'Stairway To Heaven'. In stark contrast to the monolithic mayhem touted by the heavy metal minimalists, 'Stairway' builds from a quiet elegiac introduction with acoustic guitar, double-tracked recorders and a plaintive vocal from Plant through a 'soft rock' segment to a thunderous, cathartic climax. It became a model for all 'serious' rock bands to aspire to, although few, if any, were able to emulate its innate power or popularity. For over 20 years it remained the most requested track on FM radio throughout Europe and the United States.

The band's remaining albums all had their moments of glory, but they were less consistent and suffered from an identity crisis as the band veered between diverse styles in a desperate effort to shrug off their 'monsters of metal' straitjackets.

According to legend, their name had come from drummer Keith Moon of The Who, who told them that they were so heavy that they would go down like a lead Zeppelin.

His warning was unfounded for the heavier the band became, the more the fans' fervour intensified, helping Zeppelin to become one of the most successful acts in rock history. The song with which they are most readily identified is 'Whole Lotta Love', a track driven by the best-known riff in rock, a sledgehammer staccato guitar figure, familiar even to those who are too young to have heard Led Zeppelin in their heyday through its use as the theme to BBC TV's *Top of the Pops* (albeit in a bland cover version by CCS). Ironically, it's a show Zeppelin themselves were never to appear on as they refused to release any singles in the United Kingdom in the belief that the singles market was crass, commercial and ephemeral.

Consequently, their albums continued to sell well even during the punk era when the band and their brand of rock were considered *passé*.

Deep Purple (formed 1968)

For more than a decade Deep Purple held the official record for being the world's loudest rock group and they seemed to take a pride in their notoriety. They were certainly one of the heaviest of the heavy rock outfits, but they kept faith with their blues base which gave their songs a suppleness and a broader appeal than those of the more rigid riff merchants. In their former incarnation they had a couple of psych-pop hit singles in the United States with 'Hush' and 'Kentucky Woman' before ditching their singer and bass player for more down-to-earth rockers. The new singer, Ian Gillan, lacked the subtlety of Zeppelin's Robert Plant, but he had the necessary lung capacity to be heard above the power chords and one of the most formidable rhythm sections in rock.

What fired the group was the combination of combustible personalities. Guitarist Ritchie Blackmore and the classically trained keyboard player Jon Lord were continually trying to steal the centre stage from Gillan while powerhouse drummer Ian Paice and bass player Roger Glover refused to be mere foils for the flamboyant frontmen.

There had been a time when Purple might have mutated into a prog-rock outfit, but Jon Lord's pet project 'Concerto For Group And Orchestra' (1969), recorded live at the Royal Albert Hall, was not a success, whereas the uncompromising hard rock riposte, 'In Rock' (1970), was an unqualified critical and commercial hit.

'In Rock' opens with 'Speed King' and a thunderous one-chord cacophony from which Gillian belts out a succession of lines that recall rock's past glories. But Blackmore's wild distorted guitar sound and manically vibrating tremolo, Lord's wailing organ and Paice's flamboyant drum fills are pure 1970s. The album continues in the same belligerent vein before culminating with 'Child In Time', which begins on a slow burn and builds to a screaming climax.

This formula of contrasting fast and furious all-out rockers with heartfelt blues and soulful ballads was continued on a succession of albums ('Fireball', 'Machine Head' and 'Who Do We Think We Are?') which produced the undisputed classics 'Strange Kind Of Woman', 'Black Night' and 'Smoke On The Water' and sold by the truck load before personality problems and excessive touring forced Gillan and Glover to call it a day in 1973.

Various replacements came and went with David Coverdale and Glen Hughes proving particularly effective on the robust and self-confident 'Burn' (1974), but the 'mark 2' line-up, as it is known, of Blackmore, Gillan, Glover, Lord and Paice was clearly one of a kind.

Soundbite: Yes 'Close To The Edge' (1972)

The 18-minute title track to the ultimate prog-rock album has all the hallmarks of the new form and few of the failings that were to render it virtually redundant before any of the groups had been given a chance to say anything worth hearing.

As an attempt to create a new genre of 'classical rock' (or 'clever rock' as it was sometimes dismissively termed) it's an admirable and impressive effort, fully fulfilling its promise to extend the rock musician's vocabulary and create soundscapes as vivid as those of the classical impressionists Ravel, Debussy and Satie. The sequencing of song fragments into an extended suite is entirely successful and extremely satisfying as the major themes return at key moments to bring a sense of consistency and completeness.

Despite the length there is very little padding as the band flit deftly from one idea to the next, adhering to the underlying pulse which keeps the track buoyant even during the more subdued passages.

The group members prided themselves on their technical ability and together they demonstrate a consummate musicianship and also an ability to create a densely textured sound akin to orchestration, but without the luxury of a written score.

Drummer Bill Bruford gives the opening instrumental segment a jazz-rock flavour as he criss-crosses the spiralling sitar-style guitar runs with a pattern of polyrhythms, while Chris Squire punches through the fabric with his percussive bass. In prog-rock every instrument took a lead role as they would in jazz, but sometimes the rock musicians did not have the same discipline or sense of harmonic invention and would clutter the soundstage with a flurry of notes as they fought for centre stage. Fortunately the members of Yes don't do that on this track, but guitarist Steve Howe was renowned for playing every note in the scale when a short 'lick' might have been more effective. His labyrinthine solos and those of keyboard wizard Rick Wakeman (who often played his equally flamboyant figures at the same time as Howe) combine to build grand cathedrals of sound. At the climax to this track Wakeman actually wades in with a mighty church organ that one suspects was dragged in not only for dramatic effect, but to silence all opposition!

Despite all the bombast 'Close To The Edge' has all the essential ingredients that prog-rock requires. However, in the final analysis the band's aspirations were ultimately undermined by the inane and pretentious pseudo-mystical ramblings which vocalist Jon Anderson attempted to pass off as poetry. Even the other members of the band later admitted that they didn't have a clue what he was singing about! When they too indulged their instrumental eloquence to the same undisciplined degree on later albums Yes ballooned out of all proportion until the punks came to prick their over-inflated egos and put us all out of our misery.

Multi-track recording

Rock music's increasing complexity in the late 1960s and early 1970s was due to a combination of factors, the most significant of which was the development of multi-track recording. In the early days of rock all artists were recorded playing live in the studio on to a basic two-track tape machine. These mono machines were called two track because they used reels of ¼-inch tape which had two strips of magnetic particles, one at the top and one at the bottom, so that the tape could be turned over and the bottom strip used, thereby doubling the playing time. In the early 1960s when two-track stereo multi-track machines were introduced (on which the two tracks could be used separately without turning the tape over and then played back together in perfect synchronization) bands such as The Beatles would record the instruments all together on the first track, then rewind the tape and record the vocals on the second. The Beatles' early stereo albums can be a bizarre experience for the listener who switches between channels as the unaccompanied vocals will come out of one speaker and the the vocal-less backing out of the other!

By the time The Beatles were ready to experiment with exotic instrumentation, backward sounds, tape loops and odd combinations of instruments for their ground breaking 'Sgt Pepper' album in 1967 the more flexible four-track stereo tape formats were available. Curiously, The Beatles still chose to record the main instruments live on track one and then the vocals on a separate track, leaving just two for both over-dubs and effects. At that time four-track machines were seen primarily as offering more control over the individual instruments, giving better separation and thereby a cleaner, more spacious and superior sound, but for the prog-rock bands who were restless to break out of the restrictive pop format multi-tracking offered a seemingly infinite variety of possibilities for group orchestration.

By the early 1970s technology had improved at a rapid pace to give 8, then 16, and 24, track recording on 2-inch tape which encouraged the practice of recording each instrument on a separate track (the drums being split into their component parts). This allowed each instrument to be re-recorded in the event of a mistake or technical problem without having to recall the band to re-record the whole song. It also made possible the practice of 'punching in and punching out' to patch a short phrase or even a single wrong note. Building tracks layer by layer in this fashion led to more polished, note-perfect productions, but it could be argued that it also took some of the spontaneity and raw energy out of the performance.

Having the instruments on separate tracks also meant that they could be treated individually; the tone altered with varying degrees of bass, middle and treble; and a different amount of echo or special effect applied to each. As long as the instruments had been recorded 'dry' any number of sound combinations could be created when it came to the final mix and the best mix then selected to taste. If an instrument was thought too loud it could be turned down in the mix, 'panned' to one side or the other of the soundstage or treated with different levels of echo to give the impression of it receding into soft focus while still having a presence. By being able to alter the tonality of each instrument and the balance between them, artists and producers had as wide a range of sounds, shading and dynamics at their command as an orchestral arranger and as varied a palette of colour as an artist in any creative medium.

Unfortunately, more choice inevitably led to procrastination and self-indulgence. Bands were beginning to spend months in the studio to make an album during which time it was not unknown for the initial spark of inspiration to have been entirely extinguished and the once-spirited backing tracks swamped in layers of glutinous over-dubs.

In the 1950s a band would walk out of the studio after a typical three-hour session with up to half a dozen songs 'in the can' and more often than not have two or three different takes of the same song to choose from. By the 1970s an eight-hour session was standard and was considered a success if by the end of the day the drums had been finalized on two or three songs. By the end of the decade many producers would declare themselves satisfied if they had finalised the programming of the drum machine on one song and were hopeful of completing all the drum tracks for an album at the end of the first week. But by the end of the 1970s rock was a multinational mega-buck business and each record was seen as a major investment.

The magic is in the mix

The one certain fact about mixing is that although it is possible to teach someone how to use a mixing desk, how to ensure all the signals are cleanly recorded and processed, successful mixing is largely a matter of talent, intuition and inspiration – plus a certain amount of common sense and a great deal of patience!

It's relatively easy to acquire the basic do's and don'ts, but in the end it's down to whether or not it feels and sounds right to the producer and the artist (assuming that they have any say in the matter).

The secret of a successful mix is *presence*. Whether musicians are recording in 'real time' or working alone with MIDI (Musical Instrument Digital, Interface) and samples, the track – be it traditional rock or ambient noise – has got to sound *alive*. Tasty sounds are not enough. To bring presence and dynamics to a track a producer in collaboration with the studio engineer will create the impression of space and depth so that sounds move in the mix. Movement preserves the spirit of the original performance – or, more importantly, the illusion of a performance, if everything was recorded separately.

The most successful producers have always been the most imaginative. They would think of their studio monitors as the left and right columns of a soundstage and alter the focus at different points, contrasting a small sound at the front of the stage with an expansive one at the rear. Take any well-produced rock or pop CD and you will notice that big sounds seem bigger when contrasted with a smaller, dryer sound. This trick also helps create a feeling of space to compensate for the 'dry' artificial atmosphere of studio recordings. More crucially, sounds of the same size tend to cancel each other out and lead to a muddy mix.

Another technique used to give the impression of a real or live performance is for the mixing engineer to repeat a technique used at the recording stage – contrasting a warm, unfocused sound, such as a keyboard string pad, against the sharp brightness of a steel strung acoustic guitar or piano. Many producers who have recorded a number of keyboards or guitars will alter the equalization to differentiate between each of these instruments in the mix, taking some top from one instrument to soften the edge while brightening another by adding a touch of treble.

If, however, it was still not happening for them then they would have to consider junking the take and face re-recording the whole track, as the Cult did when recording the album 'Electric' with rap producer Rick Rubin. Extreme though it might seem, it's often quicker to re-record than waste all the creative energy and enthusiasm (not to mention the energy and enthusiasm of those working with you) trying to put a spark into something that didn't have it in the first place. Ultimately, the art of record production is something that cannot be taught – it's down to an intuitive sense of what sounds right. No technical manual can compensate for a good pair of ears!

Classic albums

Led Zeppelin I (1969)

Many critics regard Zeppelin's second album as the classic (primarily for the inclusion of 'Whole Lotta Love'), but for sheer dynamism and emotional charge their first offering is arguably their finest. In contrast to the multi-layered pomp-rock productions of the 1970s it was recorded live in the studio in just 30 hours with only a minimal amount of over-dubs.

The album opens with 'Good Times Bad Times', an updating of their R&B roots with an insistent riff replacing the full chords and a typically frenetic solo from Page.

The traditional 'Babe I'm Gonna Leave You' gets a thorough reworking with a plaintive acoustic guitar intro and a pleading vocal from Robert Plant leading into a ominous staccato riff which suggests a repressed resentment that the earlier folk version could never have conveyed.

Then come two downbeat blues, 'You Shook Me' and 'I Can't Quit You Baby', which are among the most emotive tracks Zeppelin committed to tape. The first is distinguished by a fine organ solo from John Paul Jones and the second features Page and Plant trading lines in the blues tradition, but at the same time anticipating the demonstrative guitar–vocal duels which were to become a cliché of hard rock.

The other outstanding tracks are all originals. 'Communication Breakdown' is unleashed on an irrepressible riff which became the model for all full-tilt rockers, 'How Many More Times' re-writes Howlin' Wolf's 'How Many More Years', but the undisputed highlight is Jimmy Page's *tour de force*, 'Dazed And Confused'. The track opens with an insidious walking bass doubled by an unearthly piercing guitar while the tortured vocal leads us down into the abyss where the anguished vocalist bemoans his fate at the hands of a heartless female. Feedback and lashings of reverb and effects pedals, not to mention a violin bow drawn across the guitar strings, create an aural nightmare from which legions of Zeppelin fans were to emerge blissfully dazed and confused after submitting to the 20-minute version that became the climax of the band's live shows. No heavy metal band has ever bettered this track though many have tried. It is to Zeppelin's credit that they not only equalled it on several occasions, but some would say that they surpassed it with 'Whole Lotta Love' (a track which says all you need to know about hard rock in just five minutes) and the anthemic and perennially popular 'Stairway To Heaven'.

The Who 'Quadrophenia' (1970)

Recorded in 1973 when many thought Pete Townshend had run out of ideas, 'Quadrophenia' returned to the band's early days for its inspiration. Its central character is an angst-ridden adolescent whose volatile nature leads to periods of violence and depression. His suburban parents blame his erratic behaviour on inherited double schizophrenia (hence the title), but in truth he is disillusioned with the mod movement to which he belongs and is desperately in search of his real self. The songs are alternately tender and intense, mirroring his many moods, and are of a consistent high quality (which is all the more remarkable when you consider that this is a double album). When Jimmy is high, angry or pilled as on '5.15', 'Bell Boy' and 'The Real Me', the tracks explode, Moon's drums erupting out of the speakers with Daltrey's penetrating scream and Townshend's abrasive guitar in hot pursuit. But equally, when Jimmy is low or pensive as on 'I've Had Enough' and 'Is It In My Head?', Daltrey's vocal becomes tender, Entwhistle's 'lead' bass more lyrical, and Townshend's guitar melts into the melody.

'Tommy' was an impressive achievement, but this is the band's finest hour.

King Crimson 'In The Court Of The Crimson King' (1969)

Prior to forming the supergroup Emerson Lake and Palmer, vocalist and guitarist Greg Lake was frontman for King Crimson, a critically acclaimed prog-rock band with impressive jazz, folk and classical credentials. Great things were expected from Crimson following their appearance in front of 650,000 people at The Rolling Stones' Hyde Park concert in 1968 and the release of their debut album, but after Lake's departure they lost interest in conceptual rock. Instead they turned inwards to explore the infinite possibilities of jazz–rock fusion and extended instrumental experimentation, to the delight of the hardcore fans and the bewilderment of everyone else.

Their debut album, however, remains a masterpiece. It is the epitome of prog-rock with its pretensions towards art, its visions of a fantasy kingdom that bears no relationship to the real world and its impressive displays of instrumental excellence.

An album of incredible diversity, it opens with a crunching paean to paranoia, '21st Century Schizoid Man', featuring an electronically distorted lead vocal and rasping saxophones. Then, as the dust settles a flute introduces the melancholic 'I Talk To The Wind' which in any other context would have been categorized as folk. The fantasy theme continues on 'Epitaph' with a soundscape that is given a pastel hue by the ethereal string sounds of a mellotron against which Luke's mellow vocal involves visions of crumbling palaces, ageing prophets and decaying grandeur.

The wispy folksiness of the next track, 'Moonchild', precedes 'The Dream', the album's only low point, a protracted, formless and self-indulgent guitar instrumental. But all is redeemed in the majestic closing track, 'The Court Of The Crimson King', with its soaring mellotron and quirky woodwind minuet for marionettes and lyrical allusions to jugglers, jesters, witches and the other characters of this crumbling kingdom.

Black Sabbath 'We Sold Our Souls For Rock And Roll' (1976)

'What is this that stands before me?' gasps Ozzy Osbourne on the title track of the Sabs' eponymous debut album. And well he might, for the awesome package before us is a collection of their 'Satanic Majesties' most diabolic offerings culled from their first six LPs.

Beginning with that apocalyptic scene setter from the first LP and taking in a formidable offering of fiendish themes from their most productive period, this compilation proves that Britain's premier heavy metal outfit were more than Neanderthal, riff-pounding pioneers. Although they did on occasion produce the kind of thick, plodding metal for which they were constantly condemned (i.e. 'Electric Funeral', 'Iron Man'), for the most part they created strongly melodic rock and showed admirable versatility. The softer acoustic side of Sabbath as exemplified by 'Planet Caravan' and 'Changes' is light years ahead of the contrived AOR (Adult

Orientated Rock) anthems their disciples offered between unrelenting riffing.

Sabbath were never content just to invoke a bone-crushing riff and work it to death. Their best tracks switch riff, rhythm and mood more often than they later swapped lead singers. Neither were they without humour, as witnessed by the tracks 'Fairies Wear Boots' and the perennially popular 'Paranoid' in which Ozzy asks 'Are you from my brain?' with his tongue firmly in his cheek. Dementia can be fun.

Anyone who believes that heavy metal bands are in league with Beelzebub and are vile corrupters of the nation's youth should be made aware of Ozzy's candid admission that he and the band had to sleep together in the same room after seeing 'The Exorcist' – 'that's how black magic we were!'

No matter how many times their albums are repackaged they will never lose their impact as monolithic milestones in the dark history of heavy metal. If the Sabs did indeed sell their souls for rock and roll it was certainly worth it.

Genesis 'Selling England By The Pound' (1973)

'Selling England By The Pound' was the fourth offering from public school prog-rockers Genesis, a band who brought both a sense of theatre and a quirky English humour to rock. From 1967 until August 1975 they were led by the charismatic Peter Gabriel, who would appear on stage in papier-maché masks and pancake make-up to act out the characters and add narration between the songs. The undergraduate Monty Pythonesque humour didn't always raise a smile, but when it did, it set the band apart from their furrow-browed contemporaries such as Yes and Pink Floyd, whose singular lack of humour make some of their albums very heavy going indeed.

Whereas the band's first albums 'Trespass', 'Nursery Cryme' and 'Foxtrot' are richly textured (some might say 'over-produced'), 'Selling England' is somewhat simplified. The music is still very orchestrated, but it's not as grandiose and overpowering as on the earlier LPs. The arrangements are more streamlined with the minimum of shifting time signatures and fragmented rhythms making it a far more accessible and 'commercial' album. In fact it provided them with their first breakthrough hit single, the charmingly nonsensical 'I Know What I Like In Your Wardrobe'.

The album opens with the most impressive of the eight tracks, 'Dancing With The Moonlight Knight'. From a simple, almost modal, medieval-like vocal and guitar introduction it builds majestically to an instrumental workout at double speed, driven by Phil Collins' flamboyant precision drumming, and is awash with an ethereal choir and flecks of searing guitar. The only stain in this otherwise glorious track is a now dated synth sound which also crops up on 'Cinema Show' at the album's close and spoils the rarefied atmosphere.

Gabriel and Collins shared the vocals on the unassuming 'Firth Of Fifth', which opens out into a beautiful instrumental built around a rippling piano, breathy flute and soaring lead guitar which recalls King Crimson in their more pastoral moments. The similarity of their voices led some to believe it was Gabriel alone who sang. Collins' solo on the bland 'More Fool Me' shows just how close in pitch and delivery they were and in many ways offered a portent of what was to come.

Despite its title the next track, 'The Battle Of Epping Forest', had little to do with eco-warriors but instead commemorated a vicious punch-up between two rival London gangs and gave Collins the opportunity to demonstrate his talent for mimicry. In all honesty the penultimate track, 'After The Ordeal', could have had almost any title as it is a pleasant instrumental with no particular theme but enough twists and turns to please the fans who revelled in the band's cleverness. Then it was back to bemoaning the quaintness of the English character with the closing 'The Cinema Show' as a suburban Romeo romances his Juliet with a box of chocolates and she plays the demure English rose behind dabs of cheap perfume.

ELP 'Brain Salad Surgery' (1973)

ELP were at times tasteless, self-indulgent and unforgivably pretentious. Encouraged by the climate of the early 1970s, they believed that nothing succeeded like excess. But beneath the preposterous showmanship and demonstrative displays of instrumental virtuosity were a wealth of sound musical ideas, and some of the best of those were included on this album.

Of all their albums, 'Brain Salad Surgery' has the least surplus fat. 'Jerusalem', 'Still … You Turn Me On' and 'Karn Evil 9' are among their most accessible tracks, and although the Moog and organ sounds have dated considerably, it has to be admitted that their remarkable musicianship most definitely has not.

Pink Floyd 'Dark Side Of The Moon' (1973)

Of all the concept albums released during the self-indulgent 1970s 'Dark Side Of The Moon' must qualify as the bleakest. One would have imagined that its central themes of disillusionment, madness and death would have turned off even the most faithful Floyd fan, most of whom were students or ageing hippies, and yet it sold over 19 million copies and remained in the US album chart for more than 11 years.

The music is a finely judged blend of post-psychedelic art-school pop and ambient mood music which greatly appealed to students and anyone under 30 who had outgrown commercial chart pop but was not yet ready to take the plunge into the classics. It was an album perfectly in tune with the times in that it was earnestly analytical and cripplingly self-conscious, and took itself very seriously indeed.

The songs melt seamlessly into one another so that the listener is discouraged from dipping in to sample a favourite track, but is instead encouraged to appreciate the whole experience. It begins with a collage of sound effects; a pounding heartbeat, ticking clocks and manic laughter and ends with a female soprano wailing wordlessly in pseudo-operatic vein against a portentous backing on a track titled 'The Great Gig In The Sky', which all seemed very significant at the time, but in retrospect sounds merely clever and well produced. In between, bass player and lyricist Roger Waters intones his observations on the futility of life in a world-weary voice, while guitarist Dave Gilmour tears through the gossamer fabric that they wove with a lyrical line or a searing solo of burning intensity alternately.

In between the songs are special effects, footsteps, manic laughter and even a crashing aeroplane whose speaker-rattling rumble was considered to be the ultimate test of the hi-fi. For that reason and its intellectual pretensions 'Dark Side Of The Moon' was the album you played to impress friends or to convince yourself that you had finally entered the adult world.

Jethro Tull 'Aqualung' (1971)

After the wholesale slaughter of rock's 'dinosaurs' by the punk bands it became fashionable to condemn groups such as Jethro Tull and Pink Floyd as hopelessly outdated, over-inflated bores simply because they were products of the hippy era. Tull attracted more flak than most after 1976 because their folk-rock roots and over-reliance on complex time signatures made them particularly easy targets; folk being a perennially unhip and indefensible form as far as the British music press are concerned. But at their peak the band were seen as intelligent, eloquent and musically accomplished.

'Aqualung', the most consistent of a string of fine albums recorded between 1968 and 1978, considered the hypocrisy of institutionalized religion and the fate of social outcasts as personified in the tramp of the title. But even if some of the critics felt uncomfortable with frontman and flautist Ian Anderson's acrid attacks on religion, few could deny the extent of the band's musical vocabulary and the strength of the songs, specifically 'Cross Eyed Mary', 'Locomotive Breath' and the title track.

Mike Oldfield 'Tubular Bells' (1973)

The initial hype and inevitable backlash which accompanied the release of Mike Oldfield's multi-layered solo instrumental album have obscured its true significance in the story of rock. At the time it was seen as positively the last word in prog-rock, a form that had by 1973 exhausted its repertoire of grand empty gestures and shallow student philosophy. It was hard to imagine how any act could top Oldfield's achievement, which involved the 20-year-old multi-instrumentalist laying down a staggering 1,000 individual over-dubs over a six-month stint in the studio!

The format of 'Tubular Bells' is essentially classical with two long pieces of sustained invention growing organically from a simple theme which is developed, inverted and varied as other instruments are added to the mix. But unlike 'traditional' classical music the original theme is repeated throughout the piece as if played on a tape loop so that the overall effect is almost hypnotic. However, unlike either classical or minimalist music Oldfield's extended suites have a distinct rock element with a bass guitar figure emphasizing the regular rhythmic pulse and a swathe of heavily distorted guitars adding adrenaline whenever he suspects the listener's interest might be beginning to flag.

It was a remarkable achievement by anyone's standards and it helped to create a new genre of instrumental meditative music which has been called New Age, although it was actually closer to the concept of what later became known as minimalist music, as exemplified by Michael Nyman and Philip Glass.

Ironically, 'Tubular Bells' had such a profound impact on the popular imagination as being the first classical-rock 'crossover' album that it obscured the fact that Oldfield went on to make a couple of musically superior albums, 'Hergest Ridge' (1974) and 'Ommadawn' (1975), which only the hardcore fans would be playing today.

Ten essential prog rock and hard rock CDs

   1 Cream 'Wheels Of Fire'
   2 Led Zeppelin 'Remasters' (two CDs)
   3 Pink Floyd 'Dark Side Of The Moon'
   4 Deep Purple 'Machine Head'
   5 Black Sabbath 'We Sold Our Souls For Rock And Roll' (two CDs)
   6 King Crimson 'In The Court Of The Crimson King'
   7 Yes 'Close To The Edge'
   8 Genesis 'Selling England By The Pound'
   9 Jethro Tull 'Aqualung'
   10 The Who 'Quadrophenia'

7 | STACK HEELS AND SEQUINS – THE 1970S PART 2

In the cultural vacuum that was post-Beatles Britain, when rock was getting a shade too self-conscious for comfort, glam rock fulfilled a need in the neglected prepubescent audience for good-time, melodic pop with a sly, sensual smile, a self-confident swagger and a brash sense of style.

While the likes of ELP, Yes and Pink Floyd were confusing creative freedom with self-indulgence, artists such as Marc Bolan, David Bowie, Slade and The Sweet went back to basics, rejecting the idea of the pop star as virtuoso, guru and political activist and instead revelling in the role of teen idol, not caring for a moment how ridiculous they might look strutting on stage in skyscraper-high stack heels and sequins.

The music they made was never intended to last, it was ephemeral and above all it was fun, but because of its conspicuous lack of artifice it can still raise a smile and fill the dance floor when played at parties.

Marc Bolan (b.1947 d.1977)

Bolan was one of the great mythic figures of the rock era, though the myth was largely of his own making.

In 1967 this cocksure cockney kid with a staggering self-belief and an ambition to be recognized as Britain's finest pop poet hitched a lift on the hippies' magic carpet with a battered acoustic guitar and a well-thumbed copy of Tolkien's *Lord of the Rings* for inspiration. Together with bongo player Steve Peregrine-Took he produced three richly exotic acoustic albums under the name Tyrannosaurus Rex, each bursting with Eastern promise, before ditching Took for the equally striking Mickey Finn and finally plugging in his electric guitar.

For a time Bolan was lauded as an elfin-like emissary of the British underground movement. However, the hippies were not good record buyers and Bolan became convinced that there was no future for him in sitting cross-legged on a Persian rug mumbling unintelligible paeans to Pan. He ached to be a rock star and in mid-1970 he reinvented himself as the 'bopping elf', the self-styled saviour of pop. He abbreviated the group name to T Rex and pared down his music to the essentials. The result was a series of monster-selling hits – 'Ride A White Swan', 'Hot Love', 'Get It On', 'Jeepster', 'Telegram Sam', 'Metal Guru', 'Children Of The Revolution', 'The Groover' and '20th Century Boy'.

For the following three years Bolan became the focus for fan adulation on a scale not seen since the mid-1960s. Pouting, preening and posing both on-stage and on record, he seduced a generation.

At the peak of his popularity Bolan had a staggering 3.5 per cent share of total UK record sales. But this was largely from singles. He could not sustain similar success in the 'adult' album market where his contemporaries David Bowie, Pink Floyd and Led Zeppelin were to sell steadily over several decades. With stiff competition in the singles market from Slade, The Sweet, Gary Glitter, David Bowie, David Cassidy and The Osmonds, the prepubescent punters were simply spoilt for choice and Bolan was dethroned. He attempted a comeback as the Godfather of Punk a few months before his death in a car crash, but it was only posthumously that he returned to favour, becoming a cult figure like his hero Eddie Cochran.

Although few major artists have covered his songs, Bolan's attitude and spirit has been assiduously mined, as if it was the mother lode, by the prime movers of the 1980s and 1990s – The New York Dolls, Blondie, Billy Idol, Siouxsie and the Banshees, Bauhaus, REM, Guns N' Roses, Morrissey, Suede, U2 and Oasis (who, incidentally, copied the riff to 'Get It On' for their track 'Cigarettes And Alcohol'). All of them are self-confessed Bolan fans. Time, a certain nostalgia and Bolan's premature passing have burnished his early 1970s singles with a glow that would have confounded his original teenybop audience. But he was always much more than the androgynous corkscrew-haired prince of panache, a part he played to the end. He was a songwriter of unrivalled imagination and

originality and a charming fantasist. His problem was that he was
seduced by his own image. Bolan's greatest creation and most
successful fantasy was himself.

David Bowie (b.1947)

David Bowie is one of the most colourful and influential figures in
a business with more than its fair share of larger-than-life
characters and he remains as enigmatic and magnetic as an old-time
Hollywood legend. His sense of theatre and restless search for the
perfect persona may have originated from a fear of losing his own
identity through the mental illness that afflicted his mother and
step-brother, but it ensured that he became the ultimate icon of the
fragmented and self-analytical 1970s.

Curiously, the man they called 'the chameleon of rock' auditioned
a considerable number of alter egos before committing himself to
playing the part that would bring him fame and a certain notoriety.
At one time or another during the 1960s he toyed with being an
R&B singer in the Jagger mould, then a mod, a Tommy Steel
soundalike, a hippy and a mime artist before settling down to be an
offbeat singer-songwriter in the shadow of his friend and mentor
Marc Bolan. Between 1969 and 1971 when Bolan's star was in the
ascendant the pair played on each other's records, but then in 1972
Bowie took Bolan's androgynous image to its extreme to end two
decades of the mean and moody stereotypical rock star.

Bowie's predilection for wearing dresses and sporting carrot-
coloured hair may have been a ruse to secure the media's attention
but his bisexuality was not simply a pose, it was as integral an
element of his music as the science fiction themes which gave his
albums a decadent futuristic ambience.

He had been dismissed as a one-hit wonder after failing to follow
up his first UK top ten hit in 1969, 'Space Oddity', but three years
later he returned to the SF theme with the album 'Ziggy Stardust
And The Spiders From Mars'. Ziggy was to be Bowie's first and
greatest creation, an egotistical rock star with a self-destructive
streak. Fortunately Ziggy recorded one hell of an album before he
committed 'Rock And Roll Suicide', to quote the final track on the
record (see 'Classic albums' at the end of this chapter).

As far as the fans were concerned Bowie and Ziggy were one and the same, which made their disappointment all the more poignant when Bowie announced his retirement after only one year in the role. But if Ziggy had burned himself out, Bowie had not and he was back in 1973 in the guise of 'Aladdin Sane', a far more neurotic character whose album of the same name described a bleak post-apocalyptic American landscape with a harsher sound than the polished production values which made 'Ziggy' so palatable.

The apocalyptic imagery was sustained and even intensified on the follow-up 'Diamond Dogs' (1974), which saw the Aladdin Sane figure mutate into a cross between an ageing rock star and an alien in an Orwellian landscape. It took decadence and decay as far as one could go and a new persona was called for. But before he stripped off the make-up for the last time Bowie reprised the role in Nic Roeg's SF movie *The Man who Fell to Earth* (1975), a part that he might have been born to play, although in all honesty he should have played it with a bit more conviction.

By this time he was the biggest rock star on the planet and perfectly placed to revive the careers of his own heroes Lou Reed and Iggy Pop. He produced albums for both while reconsidering his position in the pop world. When he re-emerged with the album 'Young Americans' in 1975 it was as a white soul singer, although sadly not in the company of Stax or Atlantic session men, but with a sterile substitute. Bowie called it 'plastic soul', although it was more accurately described by one writer as 'the processed cheese sound of Philadelphia' (Philadelphia being the home of a particularly bland form of disco music as well as the name of a cheese spread). In comparison with the soulless dance-floor fodder that was dominating the discos and the airwaves across Europe and the United States at the time Bowie's brand of dance music sounded chic and streetwise. But it was also rather shallow and evidently unsatisfying for he abandoned it in the wake of punk and retired to Berlin in search of inspiration. The result was the sleek monochrome electro-pop album 'Station To Station' (1976) which betrayed the influence of German electronic trio Kraftwerk and saw Bowie moving further and further away from conventional rock, although the strength of the songs ensured the album was a commercial success.

The uniquely surreal atmosphere of West Berlin made a profound impression on Bowie, whose next three albums 'Low' (1977), 'Heroes' (1977) and 'Lodger' (1979) saw him stepping away from the microphone into the shadows to dabble with ambient, experimental electronic music with ex-Roxy Music keyboard wizard Brian Eno and King Crimson guitarist Robert Fripp. On 'Low', the first and best of the trio, Bowie's vocals were at a minimum and the atmosphere was all. It was a stark and strangely beautiful album which was to inspire a generation of musically untrained but enthusiastic wannabes, from Gary Numan and The Human League to Joy Division, to take to their keyboards as previous generations had taken to guitars and provide the soundtrack for much of the 1980s.

Bowie went rapidly off the boil after 'Low' with the exception of the magnificent 'Scary Monsters' album and its hit single 'Ashes To Ashes' in 1980. It was almost as if he had exhausted himself trying to top his own remarkable achievements, but for almost a decade he had either anticipated or instigated major trends in pop. He produced so many indispensable songs that two CD retrospectives were needed to cram them all on although, ironically, he sold more records in the 1980s when his influence was on the wane than he had during his 'golden years'. In 1997 he became the first rock star to 'float' himself on the Stock Market, netting a cool £500 million.

Roxy Music (formed London 1971, disbanded 1983)

When former art teacher Bryan Ferry formed Roxy Music (whose name was intended to evoke 1930s Art Deco kitsch) he intended that the group should encompass a multitude of seemingly contradictory styles and carry them off with conviction and panache. A mutant hybrid of glam and prog-rock, Roxy established a new genre which wilfully defied categorization but took a perverse delight in being alternately stylish and experimental, rockist and romantic, nostalgic and futurist and occasionally all at once.

Their eponymous debut album, 'Roxy Music' (1972), went some way towards fulfilling that promise, displaying a remarkable diversity of modes and mood while clearly being the work of one band. The tracks 'Sea Breezes', 'Ladytron', 'Re-make', 'Remodel' and their first hit single 'Virginia Plain' contrasted 1930s-style ballads and brash 1950s rock with a hint of late 1960s decadence in the manner of the Velvet Underground, the whole gilded with electronic embellishments and packaged in 1950s B-movie science fiction chic. The critics savaged the band's contrived high camp, glam image and their Pop Art pretensions but failed to single out Ferry's highly distinctive vocal style, which is one of the most perfectly 'manufactured' voices in rock, a cross between a 1950s crooner and a black soul singer.

However, all reservations were swept aside with their second LP, 'For Your Pleasure' (1973), which Ferry described as 'the one that captured what I wanted to do most clearly' (see 'Classic albums').

Roxy then moved further into the mainstream with 'Stranded' (1973), which saw the departure of Eno and the introduction of electric violinist and keyboard player Eddie Jobson. Eno's influence can still be heard on the quirky 'Amazona', but the exotic element was gone for good. The tacky trappings of glam were dropped in favour of what Ferry called the 'Casablanca look', allowing him to adopt the attitude of the fatalistic romantic, although his superficial sophistication owed more to the world-weary Noel Coward. In keeping with his new lounge-lizard persona Ferry professed that he found it easier to write sad songs and came up with the perfect pastiche in the alternately wistful and grandiose 'Song For Europe', complete with a coda in French and Latin. It would have made a classic single but the more conventional rock track 'Streetlife' was felt to be more 'immediate' and was issued instead. Two other standout cuts on 'Stranded' were 'Psalm' and 'Mother Of Pearl', the former in the 'Song For Europe' mould, strident and appropriately hymn-like, the latter the confession of a bored party-going sophisticate. The cocktail-rock image was coming to the fore.

The choice of title for the next album was further evidence of Ferry's ambivalent relationship with the smart set. 'Country Life' (1974) was an obvious dig at the select UK magazine of the same name, substituting two scantily clad females for the magazine's staid country house covers, and yet Ferry clearly harboured aspirations to be a socialite. The album consolidated the band's standing in the rock establishment with the perfectly crafted pop of

'All I Want Is You', the medieval-flavoured 'Triptych' and the Germanic cabaret-styled 'Bitter Sweet', but Roxy had lost their edge.

Its follow-up, 'Siren' (1975), was the first album to indicate a shift towards dance-orientated tracks with 'Both Ends Burning' and 'Love Is The Drug' typifying the new approach. The enthusiastic reception given to the album in America by the all-important AOR radio stations, which were increasingly dominated by disco, persuaded Ferry that the dance market was too large to ignore and that he should drop all pretensions towards art rock in favour of dance if he wanted Stateside stardom. For that reason 'Siren' was the last 'true' Roxy Music album. After its release the band split up, leaving Ferry to pursue a solo career with varying success. When Roxy reformed in 1979 they did so without Eddie Jobson and forsook their earlier innovative ideals in favour of listless dance music. Paradoxically, the blander their albums, the more successful they became.

'Flesh And Blood' (1980) is typical of this later period – all sheen and little substance. It was also their most commercially successful record, reaching number one in the United Kingdom and remaining in the charts for a full year. Highlights include the languid elegance of 'The Same Old Scene' and 'Over You', the former built on a drum machine pattern and both driven by a smooth dance beat. Other instruments are blended into the background, breaking out only for the occasional muted solo. Roxy were essentially a setting for Ferry's vocal, the ideal background for dinner parties and discos. Ferry had achieved his ambition. Roxy had become a 'class act'.

Soundbite: The Sweet 'Ballroom Blitz' (1973)

'Are you ready Steve?' – 'Uh-huh', 'Andy?' – 'Yeah', 'Mick?' – 'OK', 'Alright fellas, let's goooo!'

From the camp call-to-arms in the opening bars it's clear that The Sweet had their tongues firmly in their cheeks when they came to make this classic bubblegum single. As with all their other big hits it had been penned by the infallible hit-making team of Mike Chapman and Nicky Chinn who knocked off numerous three-chord classics for leather-clad rocker Suzi Quatro and retro-rockers Mud, many of which sounded like a Presley pastiche.

Under the make-up and outrageous costumes The Sweet were a frustrated hard-rock outfit who played the role of camp followers to Bowie and Bolan, with reluctance, because it brought them hit after hit, but they insisted on beefing up every song that Chinn and Chapman supplied them with. This gave their singles a harder edge and it guaranteed the group a wider audience than the teenybop trade.

'Ballroom Blitz' peels off with an unusual double tempo shuffle rhythm on the drums which leaves little room for conventional rhythm guitar accompaniment, such as a riff, stab or strum, so the guitar plays choppy offbeats in the spaces, creating a chugging effect like a runaway locomotive. The verses have a similar interplay between the fracturing guitar part and singer Brian Connolly's breathless vocal. When the chorus comes it offers release after the tension of a rising chord sequence to give the impression that we've all been on a rollercoaster ride that was scary but fun.

The song is childishly simple, as were all the great glam rock singles, and it is unlikely that the group were conscious of how ingeniously they had disguised its lack of sophistication by the clever contrast of complementary phrases, but that was their genius. The best pop records have always been those that were made for fun and they endure because that sense of fun is cut deep into the groove.

Queen (formed 1971, disbanded 1991)

When Queen's flamboyant frontman Freddie Mercury died of an AIDS-related illness in 1991 at the age of 45 the length of his obituaries was dictated by the group's almost unprecedented record of success and the esteem in which the gregarious and genuinely charming Mercury was held by the entire music business. Queen's incredible popularity, which at one time threatened to topple both The Beatles and Elvis from their pedestals, has ensured them a place of honour in rock's Hall of Fame, but their sales are in stark contrast to their negligible influence on the evolution of pop.

Queen began as a cleverer-than-most-kick-ass rock band with such songs as 'Seven Seas Of Rhye', 'Killer Queen' and 'Bohemian Rhapsody', but they quickly became professional crowd pleasers, as their massive stadium staged concerts and bombastic anthems 'We Are The Champions' and 'We Will Rock You' testify.

For 20 years they enjoyed an almost unbroken chain of multimillion-selling singles and certified platinum albums, their tours consistently broke all previous attendance records in Europe and America, and they broke massive new markets in Eastern Europe and South America by being the first Western rock act to perform in Hungary and Brazil. However, the stark fact is that although they did everything bigger and occasionally even better than many of their contemporaries, not a single new band has emerged betraying their influence. Perhaps it was because they were too eclectic to be copied. Their music took in 1920s music-hall pastiches, epic rock songs, note-perfect rockabilly recreations, funky disco tracks, operatic ballads and all points in between. All were impeccable, polished productions carried off with great style and panache, but musically the band were not innovators. They instigated the age of the pop video with their promo clip for 'Bohemian Rhapsody', but the track itself was a sophisticated summing up of all that had gone before.

That ability to satisfy all tastes over the course of a single album was, of course, part of their appeal, although it cost them a great deal of credibility with their original fans, who had once taken a personal pride in the fact that the group's early albums were made without resorting to the then all-invasive synthesizers. The band had been much admired for their ingenuity in creating their heavily orchestrated sound without artificial aid. But by the late 1970s they had all but abandoned rock for the dance floor, where a synth was *de rigueur*. The other reason for their success was the abundance of talent that they were able to draw upon. Unusually all four members were songwriters and they were consistently successful songwriters at that. Their sound was instantly recognizable (despite the occasional period recreations) and was characterized by a thick veneer of multi-layered vocals (again all four sang); a larger-than-life drum sound; a highly distinctive lead guitar tone from a unique, hand-made guitar and, topping it off, Mercury's florid almost operatic vocal.

Abba (formed 1973, disbanded 1981)

After winning the 1974 Eurovision song contest with the chirpy 'Waterloo' Swedish pop group Abba went on to become one of the most successful groups of all time. With an unbroken string of 18 top ten singles in the UK chart, including eight at number one and eight number one albums plus ten US hit singles, they disproved the widely held belief that all Eurovision winners were destined to be one-hit wonders. But of more long-term significance was the fact that they shattered the snobbish idea that nothing of musical merit would ever come from a non-English-speaking country and they did it with such strongly melodic, perfectly crafted singles that more 'serious' artists such as Elvis Costello felt compelled to acknowledge their excellence.

However, when they first appeared in their satin jumpsuits and silver platform boots the double husband-and-wife team of Bjorn and Agnetha and Benny and Anni-Frid demonstrated such a jaw dropping lack of sartorial elegance and such musical banality (of the 'ring-a-ding' variety) that the critics savaged them mercilessly. It didn't help that their lyrics appeared to have been scrambled together from an English language phrasebook, but the public didn't seem to care and bought their records in the millions to make the group Sweden's largest export earner, outgrossing their country's national steel industry.

Ironically, when the pressure of global stardom contributed to the break-up of their marriages at the end of the 1970s their songs began to show a new depth. From this period songs such as 'The Winner Takes It All' and 'The Day Before You Came' were imbued with a wistful melancholy. Typically the verses would be subdued with one of the girls taking the lead vocal, but then double octaves on the piano and a swathe of layered backing vocals would sweep in melodramatic fashion to a big chorus that would become as widely whistled and hummed as any of The Beatles' hits. Their songs had a simplicity that made them universally popular, but another reason for their global dominance of the pop market was their shrewd use of the music video. It meant that they could maximize exposure for a new single simultaneously in every market in the Western world without having to tour, which, incidentally, they hated and found prohibitively expensive because of the amount of musicians they had to hire in order to reproduce the sound of their records.

By 1981 the disintegration of their personal relationships made it impossible for them to continue together as a group and they split to pursue various solo projects with moderate success.

But in 1992 an Abba 'tribute' EP by electro-pop outfit Erasure topped the UK chart and initiated an Abba revival that was to see a 'greatest hits' package, 'Abba Gold', chalk up 7 million sales. Nostalgia alone cannot account for sales of that quantity.

Disco

Disco, the dance fad which dominated the pop charts for the second half of the 1970s, was not so much about music as it was about lifestyle. Although it had grown out of the vibrant black dance culture of the soulful 1960s, by the time it had filtered through the white gay club scene it was not a genuine musical movement but more of a fashion statement – and a highly dubious one at that. The gay clubs which sprang up in every city in Europe and the US in the early 1970s as a result of a more liberal society were not so hot on the music as the black dance DJs but they still needed to feed their turntables as they couldn't afford to hire live bands to play through the night. So their demand created a market for formula white funk.

Many of the disco artists were anonymous session musicians or failed soul singers who knew just enough to get a good groove going but could offer little in the way of melody or lyrics to make their tracks distinctive. For that reason one could be forgiven for thinking that all disco music sounded the same (it did) and that it was only the critical bpm (beat-per-minute) rating that enabled the dancers to differentiate between the records. In fact, it quickly got to the point where disco records had the number of beats per minute printed on the label so that DJs could segue from one to another without the dancers noticing that the record had changed!

Disco was strictly for dancing. No one actually listened to it as music because it had minimal musical merit. The few exceptions were genuine soul stars such as James Brown and Sly Stone who were initially adopted by the disco crowd until they could create stars of their own. Of these only Chic, KC and The Sunshine Band and Donna Summer had anything serious to contribute, while Summer quickly tired of singing to a monotonous drum machine that was really little more than a metronome. Her producer, Giorgio Moroder, went on to produce several huge hits for the eccentric American pop duo Sparks whose Marx Brothers-styled humour made their disco records far more fun than the gold-medallion-and-flares brigade's. Until the film *Saturday Night Fever* (1977) brought disco to the mainstream record buyers (and revived the career of Australian 1960s vocal group The Bee Gees in the process), the main customers for disco records (which were almost exclusively 12-inch singles) had been the club DJs. The club goers were just happy to have something that kept a steady pulse for as long as their legs would last. One suspects that they would have been just as happy getting down and getting it on, as they used to say, to a drum machine and a few sound effects, which is more or less what the next generation got with techno, acid house, rave and jungle in the 1990s.

It is not a matter of musical snobbery but of fact that when disco had exhausted its extremely limited musical vocabulary it left very little worth listening to.

Reggae

Reggae, the popular music of Jamaica, was the only non-American music form to have a significant and lasting impact on post-war popular music.

It began in the 1950s when the island's youth adapted the boogie piano style of American R&B artists such as Fats Domino to the electric guitar. But in doing so they accentuated the second and fourth beats to arrive at the 'offbeat chop' that is characteristic of reggae. Initially it wasn't called reggae but 'ska', an onomatopoeic name which was intended to convey the distinctive clipped rhythm.

The pioneers of the new sound were the record producers and label owners such as Leslie Kong and dance-hall DJs like Clement Seymour 'Sir Coxsone' Dodd. The DJs soon became producers themselves as they were desperate to have exclusive sides for their sound systems. The DJs were in fierce competition with each other to the extent where one would instinctively draw a gun on a rival. This gun-toting, ganja (cannabis) smoking outlaw culture was reflected in the lyrics, as was the island's volatile political scene about which the artists and producers philosophized with passion.

When it became evident that the dancers wanted to buy records as well as tickets, Dodd and his rivals began to record local acts for release. In these early years the market was exclusively for singles. It was only when the records were exported in quantity in the early 1970s and started to impact on the European pop charts that the labels could afford to make the major investment needed to manufacture and ship LPs.

Kong discovered reggae's first international star Jimmy Cliff, while Dodd's label, Studio One, had a varied roster which included such influential artists as Alton Ellis, Marcia Griffiths, Ken Boothe, John Holt, Burning Spear, the Maytals and the Wailers.

By the time the Wailers had become a backing band for Bob Marley, Jamaica's first and only superstar, Dodd was facing fierce competition from his one-time apprentice Lee 'Scratch' Perry. It was Perry who prepared Bob Marley for the fame that he would find with Island Records, an English label who were largely responsible for introducing reggae to the rest of the world. Incidentally, Island's first international hit was with Millie Small's innocuous 'My Boy Lollipop' in 1964 on which a young Rod Stewart blows a mean harmonica! It was to be another four years before reggae made a real impact with Desmond Dekker's international hit single 'Israelites', which saw the style accepted as more than a mere novelty dance style.

But before the music could be marketed to predominantly white mainstream music buyers abroad it had to have the rough edges buffed to a sophisticated sheen. Between 1964 and 1967 ska became less frantic and adopted the heavier rock sound from the American groups. It also changed its name to 'rude boy' music after the street gangsters whose exploits with the law were often portrayed in the lyrics. Prime examples of this style were Prince Buster's 'Judge Dread' and the Slickers' 'Johnny Too Bad' and 'Rudy, A Message To You'. The last named became the staple sound of the English skinhead subculture of the early 1970s and a decade later provided a hit for Coventry band The Specials who recorded it during the 1980s ska revival – one of the most inexplicable fads in pop history.

When the violence that was endemic in Jamaica's shanty towns died down in the late 1960s reggae slowed to a more sensual shuffle beat and was given the descriptive title 'rock steady'. When it sped up again in the early 1970s it retained the emphasis on the offbeat, but acquired a lilt and a bass-heavy sound. This version was termed reggae to reflect the regular rhythm (reggae means regular). In time it became the voice of the Rastafarians, a peaceful religious sect who worshipped the Ethiopian emperor Haile Selassie as God on Earth and who became a moderating influence on Jamaican life. Part of Bob Marley's appeal was the quiet dignity and sincerity underlying his music, which was an expression of his Rasta beliefs.

Other influential artists included the perfect rhythm partnership of Sly Dunbar and Robbie Shakespeare, who lent their precision to Aswad before branching out as freelance session musicians to up the ante on records by international artists such as dance diva Grace Jones and even Bob Dylan.

In parallel to the groups the DJs began having hits of their own by imitating their black American counterparts who would rap (talking in rhythm) over the records. By using instrumental 'dubs' (remixes without the lead vocals) of the records Jamaican DJs such as U-Roy, Dennis Alcapone and Big Youth were able to ad-lib their street-corner philosophy and impressionistic poetry over the backing tracks, which gave rise to an entirely new genre called toasting, a forerunner of black American rap.

With the demand for more imaginative dubs, remixing became an art and genre in itself, its prime exponents being Augustus Pablo, Dr Alimantado, King Tubby and the ubiquitous Lee 'Scratch' Perry.

From the late 1970s reggae was in danger of becoming simply another strand in the diverse fabric of pop as white acts such as The Police, Culture Club and even The Clash assimilated reggae rhythms into their own music. The acquisition of electronic keyboards and even drum machines by some of the groups in a vain effort to make the music more fashionable put a dampener on the once incendiary spark and rendered it less vital. It seemed that the prime exponents were content to cruise on past success, having made their classic records while the next generation of Jamaican youth were more eager to get into mainstream rock where the real money and celebrity was guaranteed. Then with the death of Bob Marley from cancer in 1981 the spirit seemed to go out of the music. It could be that reggae will have to wait for the appearance of an artist of the same stature as Marley to revive it and that could be a long time in coming.

Classic albums

Various Artists 'Tougher Than Tough – The Story Of Jamaican Music'

This thoughtfully compiled four-CD box, with lavishly illustrated booklet, features a formidable 95 tracks chronicling the first 35 years of Jamaican popular music. Opening with the Folkes Brothers' 'Oh Carolina' and closing with Shaggy's revamped version of the same song, it charts the evolution of reggae from the rough-hewn upbeat, uptight skank of ska through rock-steady to raga. The inevitable ska classics by Prince Buster, The Upsetters and Dennis Alcapone are interspersed with less familiar tracks by Theophilus Beckford, Laurel Aitken and The Techniques before rock steady rubs shoulders with international pop hits by Millie, Bob and Marcia, and Dave and Ansil Collins from the early 1970s.

Reminders of the music's most influential period are represented by crucial cuts from Bob Marley, Culture, Black Uhuru and Burning Spear, while hits by Chaka Demus and Pliers, Shabba Ranks and Shaggy bring the sound and the story up to date. Unfortunately, the toasters and dub stars are conspicuous by their absence. Without the likes of King Tubby, Augustus Pablo and Lee Perry no truly representative compilation is complete. Nevertheless, this is as close to a definitive history of Jamaican music as one could hope for.

Various Artists 'Glam Slam' (1989)

Glam rock was good-time party music for teenyboppers (as reflected in the groups' outrageous fancy-dress outfits). It delivered the goods in the first few bars and kept the hooks strong and simple so that kids could chant them in the school playground. It marked a return to the pure pop of the 1950s with a strong tribal beat, joyously inane lyrics and no show-off solos to spoil the fun. As such it was primarily a single's format whose highlights are best sampled on a compilation such as this one, which brings together the raucous Slade with their stomping beat and rousing terrace chants, the outrageously camp Sweet, Marc Bolan's bump 'n' grind and the Neanderthal chants of the leader of the gang himself, Gary Glitter.

Who back in the early 1970s could have foreseen that the bubblegum singles of Chinn and Chapman, who wrote a string of hits for The Sweet, Mud and Suzi Quatro, would survive punk and the 1980s? No one at the time realized what perfectly crafted pop singles these were. Curiously, for a genre that was supposedly about visual impact and an outrageous sense of style, some of its prime exponents were conspicuously unglamorous. Balding, bespectacled Elton John, laddish Rod Stewart and even the ghoulish Alice Cooper got in on the act, while Roy Wood, the reclusive genius behind 1960s psych-pop hitmakers The Move and later ELO, hid his shyness beneath layers of make-up for the Spectorish 'See My Baby Jive' and 'Angel Fingers'.

Outrageous and ridiculous as they looked, these bands put fun back into pop when it was most needed. For those of us who grew up with them, theirs will always be pop's finest hour.

Roxy Music 'For Your Pleasure' (1973)

By the time Roxy's second album appeared Eno was using his box of electronic tricks more sparingly to enhance the dark and seductive atmosphere rather than as a leading feature. 'Do The Strand' kicks off the album in fine style with Ferry promising 'all styles served here' against a relentless rhythm and Mackay's alternately honking and squealing sax. 'Beauty Queen' slows the pace, changing the mood to one of longing and reflection ('hopefully yearning' as the lyric puts it). Its theme is one Ferry was to return to repeatedly – fashion-conscious females and the transient nature of beauty. The two styles then combine on 'Strictly Confidential' which begins as a ballad with Ferry in crooning mood, a haunting oboe in the background. It then mutates into something quite alien with distorted guitar and electric piano. The formula is repeated with equal success on the penultimate track 'Grey Lagoon'. However, the album's high point remains 'In Every Dream Home A Heartache', a *tour de force* in two distinct parts. The first creates an atmosphere of brooding menace over which Ferry describes his character's empty existence and obsession with an inflatable doll! In the second, the tension is released in a liberating surge of sound which builds in intensity through the fade. The track is all the more remarkable when you learn that it was laid down as an instrumental with no idea what the title, theme or melody line was to be. Only after the track was completed would Ferry work on the melody and lyrics. It's a thoroughly satisfying album. The changes in mood both contrast and complement each other, and there is an air of confidence and enthusiasm which Roxy's first album lacked.

T Rex 'Electric Warrior' (1971)

'Warrior' was recorded in 1971 shortly after Bolan had abandoned the fey folkiness of the Tyrannosaurus Rex records for rock and before he lost himself in the bubblegum pop posturing of 'The Slider' and 'Tanx'.

Many of these tracks were recorded live in the studio with a minimum of over-dubs, which gives them a unique, earthy atmosphere similar to the early Sun records which Marc admired and was keen to recreate. Several songs betray the fact that 'the bopping elf' had raided his record collection for inspiration. 'Jeepster' is a blatant reworking of Howlin' Wolf's 'You'll Be Mine', 'Monolith' is a flagrant rip-off of Gene Chandler's 'Duke of Earl' and 'Get It On' nods knowingly in the direction of Chuck Berry's 'Little Queenie', but he reworks the old 1950s rock clichés with such style that it only adds to the charm. Even the semi-acoustic tracks crackle with raw energy and the band's barely restrained enthusiasm for the sound that they were (re)creating.

Stevie Wonder 'Innervisions' (1974)

By the early 1970s the glory days of Stax and Motown were a memory. Black music was becoming more politically conscious, but it was also in danger of becoming segregated by commercial radio who were nervous of its more militant messages. Singer-songwriter and multi-instrumentalist Stevie Wonder was one of the few black artists to get playlisted on daytime shows and so became a symbol for authentic black pop until Michael Jackson and Prince could take up the cause in the 1980s.

Stevie had been a Motown child star in the 1960s and he would continue into the 1990s as a consistent hit maker with increasingly middle-of-the-road material, but in the 1970s he struck a happy medium between funky dance tracks and soulful pop. 'Innervisions' boasts the best of both styles with 'He's Mister Know It All', 'Don't You Worry Bout A Thing', 'Higher Ground' and 'Living For The City' on which Stevie proves to be one of the few artists to make a synthesizer sound soulful!

Elton John 'Goodbye Yellow Brick Road' (1973)

Elton was one of the biggest selling singles artists of the 1970s and one of the most popular performers in pop history. The quality of his early 1970s songs guaranteed global success, but his irrepressible showmanship and his outrageous taste in clothes (both on stage and off) catapulted him into a new superstar status that he justified and sustained for three decades.

However, he didn't appear to take himself too seriously and for that reason the critics didn't either, despite the fact that he had over 30 top 40 hits and 24 chart albums including an incredible six consecutive number one LPs. But his 1997 re-recording of 'Candle In The Wind' in tribute to Diana, Princess of Wales, eclipsed even these achievements to become the biggest selling single of all time with nearly 5 million sales.

During his partnership with lyricist Bernie Taupin between 1967 and 1976, Elton produced half a dozen quality albums in the singer-songwriter mould with fastidious production values, tasteful orchestral arrangements and backing from a group whose presence gave the tracks real clout. In the United Kingdom he was seen as having more in common with middle-of-the-road maestro Liberace than Little Richard, but in the United States he became a beloved institution thanks partly to Taupin's obsession with American mythology, specifically the Old West and Hollywood movies, both of which crop up on this surprisingly consistent double-length set. Many artists have difficulty finding half a dozen top-class songs to justify an album's release while Elton evidently had memorable melodies to spare. Of the 18 tracks only a few could be classed as fillers and there are a handful of certified classics including the perennially popular 'Candle In The Wind' (originally conceived as a tribute to Marilyn Monroe), the gorgeous 'Grey Seal', the raunch 'n' roll of 'Dirty Little Girl', 'All The Girls Love Alice' and 'Saturday Night's Alright For Fighting', plus several plaintive ballads and the tastefully understated title track.

Elton may have been a bit of a ham-fisted piano player, but he could certainly knock out a good tune. So forget the tasteless tabloid trivia about his private life, the kitsch costumes and the cocktail-lounge ballads that characterized his post-1970s work (proof if needed that a man can go flabby in more places than around the waist) – this is the album that justifies Elton's place in pop history.

David Bowie 'The Rise And Fall Of Ziggy Stardust And The Spiders From Mars' (1972)

Despite its spoof SF B-movie title this is serious space rock for the 1970s and beyond. It opens with the apocalyptic 'Five Years' in which Bowie faces the end of the world with melancholic resignation and a chilling detachment. Any other artist would have kept the track for the curtain call, but for Bowie such scenarios serve as his starting-off point. From this desperate, despairing scene he takes us through the twilight world of a fictional rock star, Ziggy, his disenchanted band and followers in the five years before the world goes out with a whimper rather than a bang.

Ziggy's defiant triumphalism rages through 'Moonage Daydream' while his fans worship their hero as some kind of cosmic god on the elegiac 'Starman'. Bowie immortalizes his friend Marc Bolan and the fan fervour that he whipped up in 'Lady Stardust', then has his alter ego Ziggy dream of stardom on 'Star', and celebrate its excesses on 'Hang On To Yourself' and the title track. From this high there is only one way out for the 'leper messiah' and that is down. Ziggy succumbs to the realization that pop is ultimately just showbusiness and self-destructs in squalid isolation on the intentionally anti-climactic 'Rock 'N' Roll Suicide'.

The 1990 re-issue adds five indispensable bonus tracks including the contemporaneous single 'John, I'm Only Dancing' (original hit version), the previously unreleased 'Sweet Head' and two original demos.

Queen 'Queen II' (1974)

It is customary for critics to choose 'A Night At The Opera' as Queen's ultimate achievement, but on closer inspection their second album is a far superior and consistent set in terms of musical invention, intricate construction and the strength of the songs. Part of the reason for the later album's unjust neglect is the fact that it has been overshadowed by the commercial success of 'Opera' which boasted the inclusion of the pseudo-operatic 'Bohemian Rhapsody' and a number of other hit singles. But from the opening fanfare created by multi-tracked lead guitars through grandiose baroque pop soundscapes to the archetypal hard rock posturing of 'Seven Seas Of Rhye' this album is by far the best showcase for the group's hybrid of styles which was later to become too diverse for their own good.

Ten essential CDs

1 David Bowie 'The Rise And Fall Of Ziggy Stardust And The Spiders From Mars'
2 T Rex 'Electric Warrior'
3 Bob Marley 'Legend'
4 Roxy Music 'For Your Pleasure'
5 Various Artists 'Glam Slam'
6 Stevie Wonder 'Innervisions'
7 Elton John 'Goodbye Yellow Brick Road'
8 Queen 'Queen II'
9 Various Artists 'Tougher Than Tough' (four CDs)
10 Abba 'Abba Gold'

8 | WHITE RIOT – PUNK IN THE LATE 1970S

Punk rock, the often crude expression of a young, inarticulate and disaffected working class, was born kicking and screaming in the back room of CBGB's, a fashionable hangout in the run-down Bowery district of New York, in 1976. The club's name was an abbreviation of Country, Bluegrass and Blues, although there was not a trace of any of these prehistoric forms in the violent, nihilistic three-chord thrash perpetuated by the likes of The Ramones, Patti Smith and the aptly named Richard Hell.

Punk was a phenomenon of the late 1970s, although it did have a tenuous link to the garage bands of the mid-1960s, in that the punk groups adopted their predecessors' enthusiastic amateurish ethic and healthy suspicion of any song which had more than three chords or ran for more than three minutes. Its credo was 'don't bore us, get to the chorus', which had been the motto of the New York Dolls, a band of 'also runs' at the fag end of glam rock who can now be seen as the missing link between the garage bands and the punks, but who had disintegrated before they could exploit their belated cult status.

The punks were equally dismissive of singers who could hold a note approximating to the tune and of bands who claimed to be able to play their instruments. Raw energy was the galvanizing force of this reactionary revolution, fuelled by a distrust of the entire music industry and a healthy irreverence for the elite rock establishment, although inevitably these outsiders would eventually become part of the new establishment.

Punk was a reaction to what its creators and fans saw as the monopolization of popular music by multinational corporations and the mass media. By the mid-1970s rock music was big business and as such record companies tended to sign only those acts which they thought would have international appeal. In such a climate every release was considered to be a major investment and few labels were prepared to take risks. Likewise, radio stations in Europe and the United States were under pressure to play safe by playlisting AOR in order to keep their ratings and their audiences, who were almost exclusively composed of young adults with 'conventional' tastes. It was a vicious circle in which the bland were leading the bland. Consequently, the airwaves and the record stores were monopolized by bands who tended to tailor their music to this undemanding market. In the latter category could be filed Fleetwood Mac (once a decent blues band in a previous incarnation), the Eagles, Steely Dan and ELO, who each racked up enough sales to line the walls of their offices with platinum discs, but whose contribution to the evolution of rock was minimal – unless you count the impetus they gave to the punks who were determined to overthrow them.

The rage of the punks was primarily directed at the big-name bands of the 1960s and early 1970s who had become cultural institutions and who were becoming increasingly distanced from their fans. They measured their success by how many artic trucks (40-foot juggernauts) were needed to take their equipment on the road and by the size of the sports stadiums that they were able to fill. If you were a fan of a name band in the early 1970s chances are you had to travel to the nearest major city to see them, queue in all weathers to pay the price of a Cup Final ticket and be prepared to view the stage through a pair of binoculars. On record these bands appeared equally distant from reality with songs in celebration of a lifestyle few of their fans could afford.

For this reason punk can be seen as a welcome shot in the arm for a tired, middle-aged music scene dominated by acts who were becoming increasingly irrelevant. When the punks started to make their own music in defiance of a convention which demanded a certain standard of musicianship, years of touring experience and a management and publishing structure to underwrite the risk, they naturally sang about what they knew and felt. It's no surprise then that their songs were full of anger, frustration and disillusionment. The Ramones joked that they were fed up hearing songs about stars with expensive cars and a model girlfriend waiting by the swimming pool and so they wrote instead about the frustrations of not having a girlfriend or a car and of having nothing to do all day because they didn't have jobs to earn the money to be able to do anything worth singing about. Boredom and 'no future' became the key slogans of punk, although there was a very lucrative future to be had for those bands who had good tunes and were prepared to compromise as punk was inevitably absorbed into the mainstream at the end of the decade. Its anti-establishment statements (spiky, garishly coloured haircuts, ripped T-shirts held together by safety pins and slogans printed from clipped-out newsprint in the style of ransom demands) became fashion items to be purchased off-the-peg from the high-street chain stores, rather than motifs of a genuine musical movement.

It may have been perceived at the time as a nihilistic anti-music movement (in fact, it was just the opposite in trying to reclaim rock from the middle-aged marketing men) and it faded just like any other fad, but it opened the door for more women in rock and it reminded everyone how vital and dangerous rock could be. On a more practical level it encouraged every kid on the block who felt the urge to form a band to have a go, regardless of their musical ability, and it threw up a host of tiny independent labels, some of whom were to have a lasting impact on the music business.

Sex Pistols (formed 1975, disbanded 1978)

Punk might have remained a cult in New York City had it not been for an enterprising businessman with an eye for the main chance. Malcolm McLaren had at one time been the manager of the New York Dolls and when they split in 1976 he returned to London to run a bizarre bondage clothes boutique in the fashionable King's Road which he named Sex with his usual characteristic subtlety. Still burning to manage a rock band, he encouraged four of the most sullen, acne-riddled adolescents that he could find to form a group which he dubbed the Sex Pistols.

Drummer Paul Cook, bass player Glen Matlock and guitarist Steve Jones were passable musicians, but singer Johnny Rotten (née Lydon) was recruited for his appearance which resembled a Dickensian street urchin with a bad attitude problem. He later claimed it was all contrived and that he had modelled himself on Laurence Olivier's over-the-top portrayal of Richard III! As for his sneering style, it made Jagger and the other rock stars sound conventional by comparison. In short, Rotten and the band were conceived as caricatures to test the gullibility of the music business which McLaren hoped would swallow the hype. He kitted out the group in bondage trousers and ripped T-shirts which were held together with safety pins, and exploited every opportunity to portray them as dangerous delinquents and corrupters of the nation's youth.

He didn't have to try too hard. In December 1976 opportunity knocked in the form of an interview with television presenter Bill Grundy who managed to provoke the band into swearing on air, an act which catapulted them on to the front pages of every national newspaper in Britain and made them Public Enemy Number One overnight. After that their tours were disrupted by last-minute cancellations as local councils refused to have punk in their town, and their records were withdrawn when they were dropped by two record companies in quick succession.

Even a change of personnel (Matlock was replaced by the ill-fated Sid Vicious) and record label (their third) couldn't lift the curse. Their provocative debut single for Virgin 'God Save The Queen' (released to titillate the tabloids during the Queen's Silver Jubilee celebrations) was denied its number one chart placing by the high-street chain stores who blacked out both title and group on their in-store listings.

In November 1977 their debut album 'Never Mind The Bollocks' came up against the same problems, forcing Virgin to successfully defend the title in court against the 1899 Indecent Advertisements Act. But within a few months of the album's release the band had come apart at the seams under the weight of righteous outrage from the moral minority and the inevitable internal squabbling. Vicious committed suicide after being involved with the death of his girlfriend, Cook and Jones went to Rio to record with train robber Ronnie Biggs before disappearing into obscurity, while Lydon had the last laugh by forming Public Image and scoring serious success.

For 20 years they were mythologized as obnoxious rock-and-roll delinquents who split before their image could be tainted by compromise. But then, in 1996, they blew it by reforming for the aptly titled 'Filthy Lucre' tour. Once they had stuck two fingers up at the rock establishment but now they were finally seen as being a part of it. McLaren's movie had summed it all up in its title, *The Great Rock 'n' Roll Swindle*. The Pistols had become a parody of themselves.

The Clash (formed in 1976, disbanded 1985)

The Clash had a musical credibility that the Pistols must secretly have envied. The band claimed to come from the concrete high-rise hells of London's Notting Hill Gate where they could hear white punk, black R&B and the Rastas' reggae sound systems simultaneously. They fused all of these elements in their albums, each of them stamped with Joe Strummer's hoarse sandpaper vocal and a tight, intimidating rhythm section that owed more to The Rolling Stones than the Sex Pistols.

Their punk credibility was later thought to be questionable, but on record at least they exemplified the punk ethic by appearing to wage war on everything that they considered contrived, superficial or dishonest. Their first single '1977' declared punk's Year Zero with the maxim 'No Elvis, no Beatles, no Stones', while other songs advocated urban uprisings ('White Riot'), or condemned the practice of restrictive radio playlists ('Capital Radio One') and the US cultural domination of Europe ('I'm So Bored With The USA'). Despite the latter sentiment they toured America incessantly in a desperate attempt to crack the second most lucrative market in the world and modified their attacks on commercial rock radio by saying that every time one of their own records was played it kept bland AOR acts like Fleetwood Mac off the air for at least three minutes!

But for all their vitriolic rage against the music machine they eventually became a part of it, working with name producers and touring as support to The Who and other dinosaurs of rock. The end came in 1985 after an acrimonious meeting between guitarist and vocalist Joe Strummer and his songwriting partner Mick Jones during which Jones announced that he couldn't write songs without first checking with his accountant, to which Strummer replied, 'Then go and write songs with your accountant.'

Soundbite: The Damned 'New Rose' (1976)

While it could be argued that the Pistols were a creation of their Svengali-like manager and that their records were contrived to sound rough and ready there can be no doubt that The Damned were the genuine article. The Damned took a perverse pride in the fact that they could barely play and often sounded like a band of over-grown delinquents who had broken into the school music room after hours and were in the process of demolishing the equipment.

'New Rose' was the first punk single and a perfect summation of all that the loutish, inarticulate hordes were struggling to spit out. It's musically primitive, intimidatingly loud and poorly recorded, but that is part of its crude and awkward charm. The song was produced by Nick Lowe whose *modus operandi* was 'bang it down and tart it up later', only in the case of The Damned he didn't bother to burnish the jagged edges.

The song kicks off with vocalist Dave Vanian quoting from a 1960s girl group single, 'Leader Of The Pack', to give the nod to those in the know that we're into kitsch drive-in B-movie, schlock-horror imagery and not the serious stuff touted by the Pistols or The Clash. Then the drums pound out a tribal beat before a buzzsaw rhythm guitar grinds through the simplistic chord changes.

It's a mad dash for the fade out as the band speed on their own adrenaline for 2 minutes 40 seconds, thrashing out a corrupted version of the cliché rock 'n' roll riff once perpetrated by the likes of Status Quo, but here at ten times the speed and to far greater effect.

Several times it sounds as if the track is on the edge of disintegrating, but it just manages to pick itself up and stagger on like a drunk who's trying to carry a song that he can't quite remember. In true punk tradition there are no solos to get in the way of the penny plain verse-and-chorus structure which boasts of having no more than three chords between them. Instead the drums and guitar repeat the intro to give a break from Dave Vanian's stuttering double-tracked vocal before the band run out of steam and the whole thing shudders to a chaotic climax.

Classic albums

Various Artists 'The Best Punk Album In The World ... Ever' (1995)

Although punk was the very antithesis of glam, the two forms shared one thing in common – both considered the three-minute single to be the ideal medium with no room for surplus fat or self-indulgence. For that reason they are best sampled on a compilation such as this one which is a collection of 48 essential punk singles, most of them British but with a smattering of seminal American acts.

Disc 1 boasts the Sex Pistols' anthem 'Anarchy In The UK', The Buzzcocks' quirky 'Ever Fallen In Love (With Someone You Shouldn't've)', The Undertones' 'Teenage Kicks', The Damned's 'New Rose', The Ramones' 'Sheena Is A Punk Rocker', Iggy Pop's 'The Passenger' and a clutch of New Wave artists such as Elvis Costello, Blondie and mod revivalists The Jam. Disc 2 is equally strong with another contribution from the Sex Pistols – 'God Save The Queen', plus The Adverts' 'Gary Gilmore's Eyes', Talking Heads' 'Psycho Killer', Jonathan Richman's 'Roadrunner' and Stiff Little Fingers' 'Alternative Ulster'. To borrow a cliché, the credits read like a who's who of the 1976/77 punk scene, but are also a timely reminder of how good these bands were.

It is equally sobering for anyone who belonged to Richard Hell's 'blank generation' to reflect how these once 'subversive' songs now sound comparatively conventional and that many of those which survived did so by virtue of their self-effacing humour, a quality not normally associated with punk.

An indispensable album.

The Buzzcocks 'Singles Going Steady' (1981)

Although not strictly an album, this collection of perfect pop singles has got to be on every serious music lover's 'most wanted' list. In the white heat of the summer of 1976 the very name of the band must have sounded like a threat, but what the punters discovered to their delight was that Manchester's answer to the Sex Pistols were more subtle with their sarcasm and considerably more tuneful than their southern counterparts. While the Pistols and The Clash could be as vitriolic and intimidating as a drunken lout with a broken bottle, The Buzzcocks' singer Pete Shelley simply bitched about being a bored teenager in a whingeing voice that made him sound like the Peter Pan of punk.

He was also an exceptional tunesmith who celebrated teenage angst on such minimalist gems as 'Orgasm Addict', 'Ever Fallen In Love (With Someone You Shouldn't've)' and 'What Do I Get?'

It says much for the quality of their records that their first album 'Another Music In A Different Kitchen' (1978) is equally strong as this compilation of hits. If you get the chance, buy both.

Ten essential punk CDs

1 Sex Pistols 'Never Mind The Bollocks'
2 The Clash 'London Calling' (two CDs)
3 The Damned 'Damned, Damned, Damned'
4 Various Artists 'The Best Punk Album In The World … Ever' (two CDs)
5 The Ramones 'Rocket To Russia'
6 Patti Smith 'Easter'
7 Jonathan Richman and The Modern Lovers 'The Modern Lovers'
8 Iggy Pop and The Stooges 'The Stooges'
9 The Undertones 'Best Of The Undertones – Teenage Kicks'
10 The Buzzcocks 'Singles Going Steady'

9 | BACK TO BUSINESS – POST PUNK – LATE 1970S TO EARLY 1980S

Pop had stamped its unique and distinctive style on every year since the mid-1950s with the exception of the late 1970s. At that time the music business was still in a state of shock after the punk explosion and it wasn't until the dust had settled at the end of the decade that it was possible to get a clear view of the state of the industry and make a roll call of the survivors. The only thing that can be said with certainty about that period is that it was a time of diversity and consolidation.

On the positive side there were dozens of significant new artists maturing at a good pace and establishing themselves as a new elite. Most notable among this 'new wave', as it was initially called, were Elvis Costello, Blondie, Talking Heads, The Smiths, Kate Bush, U2, The Police, The Jam and Siouxsie and the Banshees. None of these artists saw a future with the more successful independent labels that had established themselves as serious rivals to the majors (namely Factory, Rough Trade, Beggars Banquet, Mute and Stiff), but there were enough new acts who valued their independence to keep these smaller labels in business through the 1980s.

Less propitious were the number of revivals that cluttered up the charts with cover versions of old songs and which appeared to be a desperate attempt by the establishment to pretend that punk had simply never happened. In quick succession there was a rockabilly revival led by The Stray Cats and Elvis impersonator Shakin' Stevens, a ska revival fronted by Madness, The Specials and The Selecter, all released under the banner of the Two-Tone label based in Coventry, of all places, and a heavy metal revival which revived the careers of Motorhead, Ozzy Osbourne of Black Sabbath and AC/DC, which spawned a host of derivative new acts. There was even a punk revival of sorts with the advent of hardcore (which took the furious pace of punk and increased it to an incomprehensible degree). And as usual there was a cross-fertilization of the new and old resulting in mutant forms such as thrash metal. The singles charts were largely unchanged, still dominated by the superstars of the earlier 1970s (Rod Stewart, Elton John, etc.), but joined by a handful of new names. The music itself hadn't really changed, but the new vocalists tended to have an edge and an urgency that their predecessors did not possess and there was a palpable change in the atmosphere. Notice had been served that no one, no matter how established they might be, could consider themselves indispensable.

The Police (formed 1977, disbanded 1986)

In the days before Sting (aka Gordon Sumner) reinvented himself as a self-appointed spokesman for the Third World and became seriously self-absorbed he was one third of The Police and a lot more fun to listen to.

The Police emerged from the punk circuit in 1977, which probably made their music more vital and direct than it might otherwise have been, but they were never card-carrying members of that particular fraternity and, as the echoes of punk faded, the group mellowed, to the delight of their mainly teenage female fans.

Sting (bass, lead vocals and songwriting), Andy Summers (guitarist) and American Stewart Copeland (drums) were all accomplished and experienced musicians with wider interests and musical influences than the one-chord wonders with whom they shared the bill in the late 1970s. Their main interest was reggae with just a hint of jazz, which they were able to blend with seemingly effortless finesse. This mix also set them apart from every other act of the period and made the Two-Tone ska revival bands sound positively crude by comparison. In Sting the band boasted an eloquent, occasionally humorous and restlessly inventive songwriter with a habit of writing infectiously hummable hits. Their first album 'Outlandos D'Amour' (1978) showcased Sting's songwriting skills and the trio's hermetically tight musicianship which centred around the interplay between Sting's punchy 'lead' bass, Copeland's polyrhythmic patterns and Summers' sparse harmonic shadings. It also produced a hat-trick of hits, 'Roxanne', 'So Lonely' and 'Can't Stand Losing You'. In fact, they were so 'together', to use the vernacular, that they even dyed their hair the same colour!

The formula was perfected on the follow-up 'Regatta De Blanc' (1979) which featured the hot singles 'Walking On The Moon' and 'Message In A Bottle' plus the infinitely superior 'Bring On The Night' and 'The Bed's Too Big Without You' which proved that Sting's songwriting skills were maturing at a formidable pace.

A punishing touring schedule and the pressures of following two critically acclaimed albums slowed their momentum and led to a rather predictable and subdued third outing 'Zenyatta Mondatta' (1980). Its title, taken from the Sanskrit for 'top of the world', hinted at three egos in ascendance and a tendency to pretension that would blow some of Sting's solo efforts out of all proportion. But it kept the band in the public eye and in the charts with the accompanying single 'Don't Stand So Close To Me'.

In 1981 there was a return to form with 'Ghost In The Machine', a more upfront album with a denser texture and dance-floor favourites 'Demolition Man', 'Every Little Thing She Does Is Magic' and the poignant 'Invisible Sun'.

Their final statement, 'Synchronicity' (1983), was arguably their best with a glut of fine songs, notably 'King Of Pain' and 'Every Breath You Take', and a serious attempt to broaden their rhythmic base while appearing to be masters of simplicity.

Siouxsie and the Banshees (formed 1976, disbanded 1996)

A strange incandescent beauty illuminated the music of Siouxsie and the Banshees, a band who lurched across the wasteland of punk like blank-eyed zombies from a cheap horror movie to take up residence in the decaying grandeur of a halfway house dubbed goth-rock. Gothic rock was an exotic hybrid, cross-fertilized from punk and heavy rock which bloomed briefly in the early 1980s in response to the fancy-dress antics of the New Romantics. While the latter kitted themselves out in ludicrous pirate and highwaymen costumes in the manner of the bands Duran Duran and Adam and the Ants, the goth bands and their fans dressed up in black lace and crepe like extras from a 1930s horror movie. Both forms highlighted the musical limbo of the 1980s as everyone waited for the next serious phase of the pop process.

Siouxsie Sioux's transformation from punk priestess to Gothic princess began just two years after she appeared as part of the Sex Pistols' fan contingent on the infamous Bill Grundy interview. The first two Banshees offerings, 'The Scream' (1978) and 'Join Hands' (1979), were predictably bleak proto-punk albums, but the third, 'Kaleidoscope' (1980), took a detour into dark psychedelia as distilled on the singles 'Happy House' and 'Christine'.

Their fourth album, 'Juju' (1981) witnessed the beginning of their Gothic phase and could be said to have kick-started the careers of the Cocteau Twins, The Sisters of Mercy, The Mission and The Cure, to name but four. The album opens out like a dark and deadly orchid to pervade the air with the sickly sweet perfume of corruption and decay. The tracks don't grow upwards towards the light, but instead snake along the ground to the accompaniment of an insistent, ominous drone, a swarm of strings and a smattering of ethnic percussion. And gliding on top is Siouxsie's spectral, keening vocal swamped in reverb and sounding like a carnival barker announcing the attractions at her freak show.

There were other fine albums, namely 'A Kiss In The Dreamhouse' (1982), 'Peepshow' (1988), 'Superstition' (1991) and 'The Rapture' (1995), and a few inevitable disappointments before the band called it a day in 1996.

There are no happy endings or major key modulations in Banshees' songs, but a brooding fatalism, unrelenting and ultimately emotionally draining. There is a mesmerizing melancholia in their music which makes most pop sound contrived by comparison.

New Wave

The New Wave was not so much a reaction against punk as an insidious and cynical distillation of the punk ethic. It was a predominantly American movement in which bands adopted the couldn't-care-less attitude of the original punk bands and psyched themselves up to play with the same intensity, but much of it was a safe, Xerox copy for middle-class kids. The best of the New Wave bands (Blondie, The Cars and Talking Heads) made some great records and left an indelible impression because they brought something extra to the formula, but they were the exception.

Blondie initially penned strong, perky songs on kitsch B-style themes and boasted the delectable, fragile-voiced Debbie Harry whose presence ensured them maximum publicity. After breaking through with the bouncy 'Denis', a cover of a 1960s song, they became more mainstream and radio friendly until they mutated into an anonymous backing group for Harry for their multimillion selling global disco hit 'Heart Of Glass'. Harry's insistence on working with Eurodisco Svengali Giorgio Moroder netted the band their only transatlantic number one, 'Call Me', but it also strained relations within the group to breaking point and lost them the last vestiges of credibility. They split in 1982, but 17 years later they patched up their differences and reformed. Against all the odds they crashed back in with a number one single, 'Maria', sounding like a track that could have been lifted off any of their earlier LPs.

The Cars were heavily criticized throughout their career for producing emotionless pop-art songs, but looks can be deceptive. Beneath the sheen of their platinum-selling albums a rock-and-roll heart was beating. The Cars' image of slick detachment was of their own making, an image perpetuated by the use of pop-art motifs and super models on each album cover. It was such attention to style that blinded many of the critics to the quality of their songs, many of which were beefed up with a solid rhythmic punch, propelled by a clipped guitar laced with the neatest keyboard and guitar hooks this side of T Rex.

In fact, The Cars' infectious beat owed more to Marc Bolan than to The Velvet Underground or Roxy Music with whom they had been compared. In their native America they sustained their success and domination of FM radio for just over a decade, but in Europe they are chiefly remembered for their first single 'My Best Friend's Girl' (the first 7-inch picture disc) and the soft rock smoocher 'Drive' featured during the 'Live Aid' spectacular in 1985.

Talking Heads were almost unique among the class of '76 in that they retained their credibility and the respect of the capricious music press throughout their 15-year career. Without a hint of pretension or compromise they managed to appeal to both the head and the feet with edgy, intense and ironic songs fused to an irresistible dance beat and sung in a slightly manic, high-pitched voice by frontman David Byrne. While their contemporaries were speeding on their own adrenaline, Talking Heads exemplified the Zen ethic – they kept their heads when all around were losing theirs, maintaining a cool detachment and a heightened state of awareness bordering on the transcendental. But there was always a neurotic undertone which made them unpredictable and therefore extremely interesting.

The band were formed by three graduates of the Rhode Island School of Design who brought their art-school sensibilities and incisive observations on urban life to the nihilistic punk scene. Their debut album 'Talking Heads '77' (1977) preserved their most idiosyncratic song, 'Psycho Killer', while their second, 'More Songs About Buildings And Food' (1978), reduced the punk and increased the funk element under the auspices of their mentor Brian Eno. Eno also produced their third album 'Fear Of Music' (1979) which saw the band assimilate the sounds and rhythms of traditional African music. Traditional ethnic elements became increasingly important, most notably on one of their finest albums, 'Remain In Light' (1980), which spawned the global hit single 'Once In A Lifetime'.

The band produced the next album, 'Speaking In Tongues' (1983), themselves, which gave them a US top ten hit with 'Burning Down The House'. While the latter was still entrenched on the radio playlists they followed it with a superior live album and concert film (both titled 'Stop Making Sense') to prove that the increasing complexity of their music did not prevent them from being able to cut it as a live act.

It proved to be the apex of their career for after this the members became increasingly absorbed in various solo projects and the subsequent albums 'Little Creatures' (1985), 'True Stories' (1986) and 'Naked' (1988) were interesting rather than inspired. Byrne disbanded the band without apparently consulting the others in 1991.

Kate Bush (b.1958)

In 1978 the precociously talented Kate Bush arrived wide-eyed and fully formed on the British music scene with a distinctive hit,

'Wuthering Heights', and a portfolio of songs that she had been writing since the age of 12. Her winsome voice, obvious originality and apparent vulnerability charmed the critics and mesmerized most of the male population.

Her debut album, 'The Kick Inside', confirmed the advent of a major talent and the subsequent singles 'The Man With The Child In His Eyes' and 'Wow' proved her commercial potential. Her second and third albums ('Lionheart' and 'Never Forever') garnered even greater praise and healthier sales (the latter entering the UK album chart at number one) and her elaborately choreographed stage shows suggested that there was no end to her talent. But her first tour proved too arduous and she retired to her private recording studio leaving specially commissioned video clips to do the promotional work for her.

It was a strategy which paid off handsomely both in terms of increasing sales and in enhancing her image as a reclusive genius. But the more time she spent on her albums in endeavouring to integrate the latest technological toys with traditional instruments and ethnic 'roots' music, the more complex and less accessible they sounded to the average fan. Her 1982 offering, 'The Dreaming', was too densely textured, thematically obscure and self-indulgent for many, but after a three-year hiatus her fortunes revived. Her 'comeback' single, 'Running Up That Hill', marked a return to a more direct approach with its insistent drum pattern and staccato strings and the accompanying album, 'Hounds Of Love' (1985), was less ambitious but rich in imagination and diversity of material.

In the following decade her little-girl voice would begin to grate and her perfectionism would become almost obsessive to the point where she would take several years to make a new album. But the wait only served to make its release a much anticipated event and added to her mystique.

Bruce Springsteen (b.1949)

It is fitting that the coda to Springsteen's career should be the subdued, semi-acoustic album 'The Ghost Of Tom Joad' (1995), which had been inspired by a character from John Steinbeck's novel *The Grapes of Wrath*, because in the final analysis

Springsteen's work owed more to Steinbeck than Bob Dylan, with whom he had often been compared.

The man they called 'The Boss' was hyped to fame in the early 1970s by an orchestrated media campaign which drew unjustified parallels with Dylan, after which he cultivated an image as an all-American hero with the subtlety of a pool-hall hustler.

In Springsteen's songs the system was injustly harsh and always grinding the good man down. Spiritual deliverance came in the shape of a fast, gleaming automobile, an endless rolling highway and a girl to share his dreams. It was a cliché which appealed to a large, predominantly conservative section of the white male AOR audience who might have thought of punk as subversive and disco as effete.

But the wild-eyed optimism and bar-room ballads of 'Born To Run' (1975) and 'The River' (1980) all but obscured the acute observations of small-town America contained on the infinitely superior 'Darkness On The Edge Of Town' (1978), the solo acoustic 'Nebraska' (1982), the bitter 'Born In The USA' (1984) and 'The Ghost Of Tom Joad' (1995).

Springsteen may have filled vast sports stadiums through the 1980s on the strength of his bellicose anthems and his marathon four-hour stage shows, but it was his intimate, poetic descriptions of those who despaired of sharing in the American dream that ensured his place in the rock-and-roll Hall of Fame.

Soundbite: The Jesus and Mary Chain 'Psycho Candy' (1985)

Scotland's The Jesus and Mary Chain were never destined to be pop icons or even vastly influential, but with one lingering howl of feedback and a languid semi-acoustic tribute to the Velvet Underground they summed up the vain hopes of a thousand bedroom bands and were rewarded with their 15 minutes of fame.

Ten years earlier the punk fanzine *Sniffing Glue* had published a diagram of a guitar fretboard showing the finger positions for three major chords with the instruction, 'Now go and form a band'. The Jesus and Mary Chain exemplified that 'heads down and have a go' ethic, but they also prefigured the return to pop values by the Seattle grunge bands and the Brit-pop guitar groups of the 1990s.

The track starts in typical low-key melancholic fashion with a drum machine punching out a robotic rhythm rather ineffectually while a pizzicato guitar figure leads us gently into a dark and somewhat sinister world where singer Jim Reid waits in the shadows to relate his sordid tale of madness and drug addiction. His narrative is close-miked and awash with lashings of echo to give an intimate, confessional feel. Only when the middle eight comes does the track pick up tempo and Jim is joined by his brother William on second guitar and a barely discernible backing vocal. Musically, there are no surprise twists and turns, but a simple and effective contrast between major and minor chords to create a bitter-sweet sound that lingers like the brooding images in a *film noir*.

Classic albums

The Fall 'The Wonderful And Frightening World Of ...' (1984)

Behind every successful man there's a woman, or so the saying goes. Behind the sardonic and long-suffering Mark E Smith stood Brix, credited with vocals and guitar, but whose contribution extended to a total makeover of the band. Before Brix appeared centre stage The Fall were idiosyncratic just for the perverse pleasure it gave them in being different. She tightened up the rhythm section and streamlined the overall sound while allowing Smith to remain, wailing at the centre of the maelstrom a tone or two off key. The result – The Fall retained their quirkiness, the unpredictable and anarchic but appealing arrogance of their early days, but with a more conventional sound.

Their 1984 outing, 'The Wonderful And Frightening World Of ...', best exemplifies this perfect balance of hardcore punk, Performance Art poetry and aural DIY.

The opening track, 'Law Of The Land', is as dangerously close to hard rock as its companion 'God Box' is to contemporary pop, with only Mark's monotonal vocal and a brace of dubiously tuned guitars to remind us that this is indie country. In fact, the only track to sound like the disconcerting, provocative Fall of old is 'Bug Day'.

The one or two snatches of pretentious pseudo-poetry, white noise and other arty diversions are the only moments when The Fall play at being DIY darlings and fall flat on their pretensions. For the most part they are less obtuse and experimental than the music press would have us believe.

Far from being an anachronism on CD, they benefit greatly from the clarity their vinyl offerings lacked. They are less grating but no less threatening, no less challenging for being smoothed out by transfer to digital. They are indeed 'this nation's saving grace', to quote one of their other album titles.

The Smiths 'The Queen Is Dead' (1986)

Together with their Mancunian mates The Fall, The Smiths embodied the spirit of independence and integrity in a decade characterized by conveyer-belt commercialism, compromise and conformity. Their choice of name emphasized their anonymity, celebrated their Britishness and hinted at their disdain for pop's obsessions with silly and pretentious names. After refusing offers from numerous major labels they chose to remain with leading UK indie Rough Trade even when it became obvious that their popularity made such principles impractical.

The four studio albums and the 18 singles that they released over the course of four years together spent less than a month in the UK charts (probably because they steadfastly refused to make a video), but their impact and influence was considerably greater than is suggested by the statistics.

This, their third album, tones down the maudlin musings of singer and lyricist Morrissey – which were summed up in the title of one of their finest singles, 'Heaven Knows I'm Miserable Now' – in favour of sharp, sardonic observations on the English preoccupation with social proprieties and keeping up appearances.

Morrissey's cynicism and droll, deadpan delivery are set into sharp relief by the jagged guitar lines and lush melodies provided by his songwriting partner, guitarist Johnny Marr, as the pair point accusing fingers at a society obsessed with trivia and the weaknesses of others. But there is also an undercurrent of self-mockery and a generous dose of self-pity to add balm to the stinging sarcasm. The cult of the miserable continues.

AC/DC 'Highway To Hell' (1979)

An indispensable offering from those sultans of subtlety, AC/DC, 'Highway To Hell' is the perfect fusion of Aussie bar-room boogie and heavy rock riffola. The sound is crisp and even at low volume it packs a real wallop. Sadly it was the last album recorded with the late Bon Scott who was responsible for such memorable titles as 'Walk All Over You', 'Love Hungry Man' and their only UK hit 'Touch Too Much', which charted the week he died. Though live in feel there's no self-indulgent soloing here, nor any hint of the catalogue of clichés which compromised their later albums with replacement singer Brian Johnson.

If anyone still doubts that Bon Scott beats Brian Johnson hands down, this one will settle the argument. No heavy rock fan should be without a copy.

U2 'War' (1983)

This album was made in the days before Ireland's finest, U2, were lauded by some as the greatest rock band in the world and loathed in equal measure by others who saw them as superficial, pretentious, self-important poseurs. It is customary to list 'The Joshua Tree' as the band's best effort, but there is something much more appealing in this early outing when music still meant more to the band than their status as saviours of rock.

The sound of The Edge's shimmering guitar fills was a revelation at the time and Bono's passion seemed sincere, both offering much needed assurance that the publication of rock's obituaries had been premature. It is easy to hear why Bruce Springsteen, Pete Townshend and the Sunday supplements saw them as the future of rock. But it is not only the sparseness of their sound using just bass, drums and guitar which sets them apart from the over-produced electronic pop of the period, it is the commitment and idealism which shames the cynical, computer-created fodder that was then clogging up the charts. And which other album of the early 1980s could boast three anthems of the calibre of 'New Years Day', 'Two Hearts Beat As One' and 'Sunday Bloody Sunday'?

Guns N' Roses 'Appetite For Destruction' (1987)

Los Angeles band Guns N' Roses were one of those rare rock-and-roll animals that were shamelessly hyped to fame but then surprised the cynics and the critics by proving just how damn great they really were. Admittedly they carried it off just once with this, their first album – the sequels being pale imitations of the one genuine moment of glory – but it was enough to revive one's faith in the restorative power of rock.

Their image was contrived to appeal to adolescent males who were too young to remember Led Zeppelin and The Rolling Stones and their sound was a confusion of clichés with wall-to-wall guitars and singer Axl Rose affecting the mannered vocal style of a horde of hoarse heavy metal screamers. One critic accurately described him as sounding like a man undergoing surgery without anaesthetic. There was little new in their music, which was a warmed-over stew of hardcore punk and heavy metal influences, but they served it up steaming and strong.

Whatever misgivings one might have concerning their blatant borrowings it is an indisputable fact that few albums can boast a track listing as consistently exhilarating as this one. They peel off in fourth gear on the opener 'Welcome To The Jungle', cruising for a couple of tracks that would be highlights on anybody's else's album before giving it gas on 'Mr Brownstone', 'Paradise City' and 'My Michelle'. Then they cool things down with 'Sweet Child O' Mine', a classy anthem that one suspects was written just to prove that they could do it.

They may be a serious case of arrested development, but they made a hell of a kick-ass album.

Ten essential post-punk CDs

1 The Television Personalities 'Yes, Darling But Is It Art?'
2 Elvis Costello 'My Aim Is True'
3 The Police 'Outlandos D'Amour'
4 Siouxsie And The Banshees 'Once Upon A Time – The Singles'
5 Kate Bush 'Hounds Of Love'
6 The Fall 'The Wonderful And Frightening World Of …'
7 U2 'War'
8 Guns N' Roses 'Appetite For Destruction'
9 The Smiths 'The Queen Is Dead'
10 The Cult 'Sonic Temple'

10 TECHNOLOGY TAKES OVER – THE 1980S

After the austerity of the punk era there was a need for pop to be fun again. In Britain under Prime Minister Margaret Thatcher and in the United States under President Ronald Reagan the 1980s were promoted as the era of personal prosperity and everyone was encouraged to party like it was 1999.

The mainstream pop music of the 1980s was primarily party music and bands and fans dressed accordingly. But the New Romantics, as the first wave was called, didn't want to go back to the 1950s retro rock of the glam era. They saw themselves as being at the dawn of the digital age with 24-hour music television on tap from satellite, music videos threatening to replace live concerts and computer technology promising to make every hopeful amateur sound like a professional musician. They wanted to create a sound that evoked the brave new world to come, which they imagined only electronic keyboards and drum machines could produce.

For less than the price of a decent electric guitar and amplifier any teenager in the 1980s could buy a keyboard and reproduce the sound of an entire rock group at the touch of a button, with a far more authentic sound than the crude, rasping electronic synthesizers of the 1970s. Thanks to the mass production of the microchip even the most inexpensive keyboards offered the sound of real strings, pianos, drums and bass, among a range of other instruments, all of which had been 'sampled' from real instruments. You didn't have to be a real musician to sound good. You didn't even have to be able to play accurately or in time. A spot of judicious editing and the computer could be programmed to play the keyboard, a bass synth and a drum machine note perfect each and every time. Pop became programmable.

It also became predictable. The trouble was that a lot of artists were using the same keyboards and drum machines because they had heard them used on a successful recording and they wanted to sound contemporary. Pop lost the human touch and many chart records became indistinguishable from each other with only the vocal to help tell them apart.

Those who managed to establish an identity and bring some colour back into the charts during the decade included the Pet Shop Boys, Depeche Mode, New Order, The Human League, Eurythmics, Wham, The Thompson Twins, Orchestral Manoeuvres In The Dark, Culture Club, ABC, Marc Almond and Duran Duran.

Some of these made classy records while others made decent designer disco for a decade preoccupied with image. But, as always, there were new artists who dictated fashion rather than following it and in so doing determined the direction that popular music would take in the future.

Madonna (b.1958)

Madonna emerged from the New York dance club scene in 1984 with a voracious appetite for publicity, but seemingly little talent. Her first hits ('Holiday', 'Like A Virgin', etc.) were standard, updated disco numbers, her image a confusion of trash chic and her voice was accurately described as sounding like Minnie Mouse on helium.

She declared that it was her ambition to leave as indelible an impression on popular culture as Marilyn Monroe had done, and she succeeded. Within a decade she had racked up 30 consecutive self-penned hit singles, made half a dozen movies of variable quality, earned an estimated $115 million and inspired a glut of academic theses from the faculty heads of several American universities, including one entitled 'The Madonna Collection: Representational Politics, Subcultural Identities and Cultural Theory'. But she was criticized with equal enthusiasm by those who saw her as shallow, narcissistic and manipulative. Her whole life, it was said, was a performance.

It was only after her novelty was beginning to wane in the mid-1990s that she attempted to reinvent herself as a serious artist with some success. A starring role in the film version of the musical *Evita*, a series of slick, imaginative stage shows and a trio of more adult albums ('Erotica', 'Bedtime Stories' and 'Ray Of Light') suggested that she had finally grown up and had the talent to justify all the hype.

Prince (b.1958)

At the age of 19 singer, writer and multi-instrumentalist Prince Rogers Nelson was signed by Warners for a six-figure advance and given carte blanche to write, arrange, produce and perform whatever he wished without interference of any kind from the label.

The company's faith in him remained intact despite the fact that his first four albums had little impact and negligible sales.

It wasn't until 1982 when the promo video for his single 'Little Red Corvette' was playlisted on MTV that Prince became the star that he had prepared himself to be. The accompanying album, '1999' (1982), and its title track became worldwide hits, winning over a wide cross-section of fans who found its ingenious blend of black dance music, white pop and heavy rock guitar soloing irresistible. Such a mix had not been attempted since Jimi Hendrix dabbled with rock, jazz and funk with the all-black Band of Gypsies in the last years of his life. Prince's innovation was to take Hendrix's sculptured over-driven guitar sound and weld it to a range of infectious dance beats, then spice it with sexually explicit lyrics and contrast these images with a yearning for spiritual release. It was an outrageous concept and one which caught the imagination of a generation who were bombarded with conflicting messages by the media who effectively encouraged them to indulge in sexual experimentation and yet stalked them with the spectre of AIDS. Prince's message appeared to be one of reckless hedonistic excess, to 'party like it was 1999', the eve of the supposed apocalypse.

On stage Prince was surrounded by a mixed-race band with male and female members who put on a show that was visually stunning, but reminded outsiders of an extravagant Hollywood pantomime. It was a fairytale and Prince played the Principal Boy to the hilt.

The media saw him as a saviour of pop in a decade which produced few genuine stars and the fans delighted in his precocious talent, but the US pro-censorship lobby, the PRMC (Parents' Music Resource Centre), accused him of corrupting a generation. The fact that he was black and apparently of no fixed sexual orientation must have made them even more nervous.

Prince responded with an increasingly eclectic series of albums promising spiritual and sexual liberation for those who bought in to his fantasy. However, by 1993 his increasingly erratic behaviour, which included renaming himself 'the artist formerly known as Prince', and his failure to produce all of the ambitious projects with which he had teased the media led many to conclude that he had been just another flamboyant pop star who had over-stretched himself.

Soundbite: Ultravox 'Vienna' (1980)

It is almost impossible to separate the hit songs of the early 1980s from the promotional videos that helped to make them hits. Many of these three-minute clips cost more than the original recording and more than a few were heavily criticized at the time for dazzling record buyers into shelling out for substandard singles. They were created with the same fast editing techniques and effects that were used in commercial television advertisements, but not all of them had better soundtracks. A famous put-down phrase of the period summed it up, 'Nice video, shame about the song'. 'Vienna' by Ultravox was a notable exception, although those who remember it will still find it difficult to listen to the music without being haunted by the imagery of the video.

Like many of their contemporaries Ultravox were a keyboard-based band (even the drummer was a machine). As such they were too static to be filmed in performance and so for this stylish single they dressed up like extras from *The Third Man* and acted out a forgettable scenario in locations around Vienna. The video's crisp chiaroscuro black-and-white photography (shot on sharp 35mm movie film, not video tape) evoked the brooding atmosphere of the single perfectly.

The slow, ominous drum machine pattern is augmented by snare bursts in heavy reverb to generate an 'epic' feel. Against this stark backdrop and the odd pianistic embellishment singer

Midge Ure proclaims the lyrics with an almost operatic flourish that gives the words a significance they don't really deserve, but which is entirely in keeping with the grandiose ambience they are trying to create. Then as the vocal rises to the chorus there is a surge of (keyboard generated) strings and the track opens out dynamically, the vocal soaring on a single note as Ure sings the title and a bass synth drone growls at the bottom end. The instrumental middle eight then kicks in at double tempo with a sinewy solo violin before the track slows dramatically for the final chorus.

It may be contrived, but it's also cleverly constructed and stands head and shoulders above the other electro-pop hits as one of the classier records of the era.

Club culture – house, scratch, techno, rap and sampling

By the mid-1980s the sweet sound of American soul music had acquired a harder edge and a rhythmic dynamic that reflected the reality of life in the inner cities. Disco had been dismissed as passé and funk had become almost a parody of itself. Black music had been in danger of losing its soul to show business until its beat and bass lines were sampled by a new generation who were determined to bring it back down to street level.

The new sound of soul was potentized in the Bronx district of New York in the early 1980s by DJ Afrika Bambaata who wanted to make a new dance form that would appeal to a multi-ethnic audience in the clubs and also to the kids who were breakdancing to portable beatboxes in the parks.

His idea was to take the sermonizing style of the Jamaican DJs who rapped, or 'toasted', over their records and weld it to the electronic beat of German synthesizer band Kraftwerk who he believed had pioneered the music of the future. It was an unlikely partnership but it proved to be an inspired match and an extremely prodigious one.

Bambaata remixed Kraftwerk's tapes using samplers, sequencers and drum machines to create his own version of their music on a

track which he called 'Planet Rock'. With this one record he
initiated the age of the DJ as producer and created a new,
predominantly black dance form which was to mutate into a myriad
diverse dance styles including house, rap, jungle and techno.

House music took its name from the Powerhouse club on the
south side of Chicago where the resident DJs fed slickly produced
mid-1970s disco records through a MIDI computer which enabled
them to over-dub additional keyboard lines and drum fills live in
the club and in perfect sync to the beat without having to remix the
track in a studio. It effectively made new records from old to the
delight of the dance crowd, although it had little to do with creating
music as the DJs could only play simple lines in sync with the aid
of the machines. The keyboard lines were usually subterranean
wall-shaking bass figures rather than top-line melodies and there
was an emphasis on special sound effects such as 'scratching'
(manipulating two copies of the same record on the turntable by
hand). With such a limited musical vocabulary house soon lost
its novelty. By the end of the 1980s its trademarks had been
assimilated into mainstream pop by acts such as Soul II Soul, KLF
and The Shamen.

Early examples of the genre were the singles 'Jack Your Body' by
Chicago DJ Steve 'Silk' Hurley, 'Pump Up The Jam' by Belgium's
Technotronic and a more laid-back British version spun by
M/A/A/R/S ('Pump Up The Volume'), S-Express ('Theme from
S-Express') and Bomb The Bass ('Beat Dis').

Techno took over the house when the latter became passé. Techno
was an intense, 'soulless' computer-generated dance music which
had been created in Detroit by faceless (and therefore
unmarketable) whizzkids who fused hardcore funk to the electronic
noise of Kraftwerk and the repetitive sequenced bass lines of
Eurodisco maestro Giorgio Moroder. The result mimicked the
robotic, pneumatic sounds of the machines of the city's car plants
and, not surprisingly perhaps, proved particularly popular in other
industrial centres, specifically Frankfurt and Sheffield.

Techno in turn separated into two polarized camps – a more mellow
ambient form, as exemplified by bands Orbital and Underworld,
and an even harder and more frantic variation incorporating raga

reggae styles which was initially known as jungle (but renamed 'drum and bass' to avoid accusations of racism) of which the Prodigy were acknowledged as prime exponents.

Rap

Rap began in the black and Hispanic ghettos of New York in the late 1970s as a form of self-assertion by underprivileged kids who saw themselves as having been abandoned by the system. Their protest took the form of a half spoken–half sung rhyming monologue improvised over existing records in the manner of the Jamaican DJs and radical black artists The Last Poets.

The Sugarhill Gang's 'Rapper's Delight' (1979) may have been the first worldwide hit in this style, but it was not typical. Instead it was their label mate Grandmaster Flash who provided the template for the hard, intimidating soapbox style that was to dominate black music for the next two decades. 'The Message' (1982) by Grandmaster Flash and the Furious Five was a top ten hit on both sides of the Atlantic and established rap primarily as a medium for social comment.

The major record companies were initially reluctant to sign rap acts which they saw as being too politically provocative to market to the mainstream music buyers. This left the field open to enterprising independent labels such as New York's Def Jam who hooked the biggest acts (LL Cool J, Run DMC, The Beastie Boys and Public Enemy) and scooped the lucrative white suburban sales.

Rap was initially perceived by the musical establishment as being as dangerous as punk had once been and so there were no rap acts on the bill at the Live Aid fund-raising concert spectacular in 1985 and none playlisted in the early years of MTV. However, rap became increasingly predictable and by the early 1990s it had been absorbed into white pop to give a fashionable flavour to tracks by the Spice Girls and innumerable copy-cat 'girl-power' puppets and manufactured 'boy' bands.

In response, black acts split into two camps, the more militant gangsta rappers and the mellow retro-soul bands such as De La Soul.

By the 1990s dance music was no longer structured around a song, but around a few bars or a segment snipped from some other artist's record. At first artists such as Led Zeppelin and James Brown seemed to be flattered by having their old riffs and rhythms reach a new audience in this way, but then the samples became more central to the songs and the increasing sales meant someone was raking in lots of royalties from recycling other people's ideas. At least that's the way the lawyers saw it and now groups are encouraged to have a meeting with their lawyers before recording begins to make sure that the rights are settled before a single note is sampled!

What is a sampler?

Samplers are potentially the most exciting creative tool to appear since the invention of the synthesizer. Although they are, in essence, tapeless digital recorders for recording and instantly replaying snippets of sound, if used imaginatively they offer the aural equivalent of Virtual Reality to club DJs, record producers and remix maestros as well as musicians. Initially, in the early 1980s, they were used mainly by dance-floor DJs and 'underground' club acts as basic record and playback devices to copy and 'loop' riffs, phrases and hooks from other artists' records to spice up and add novelty to a dance track. But recent advances in technology now equip them to recycle sounds with the versatility of a top-flight synthesizer, so that the sound of a complete orchestra or a continuous percussion track, for example, can be triggered with the touch of a single key. Even when heard in isolation it is almost impossible to determine whether a well-sampled sound is 'real' or sampled, as the original sound sources are invariably 'real' instruments digitally recorded to avoid any taint of artificiality.

The beauty of sampling is that it enables the artists to capture the actual sound source like a butterfly in a bottle and not simply electronically synthesize an approximation of it to fool the ear, as the early synthesizers used to do. That said, samplers share some of the functions of a synthesizer in reshaping the sound once it has been loaded.

The great thing about sampling is that the artist can do what he or she likes with the sample once it is in the computer. This cannot be done with a musician who comes in to record a part on a particular track as the part will remain as it was played.

But once a sample has been digitally stored it can be turned back to front, repeated endlessly as if it was on a tape loop, and the speed can be altered. The original sampled line may have been used only once, so it is to the sampler's credit if he or she sees the potential of a fragment and uses it more prominently. Ideally, a sample should be juxtaposed with another sound to create a unique element rather than being used bare and blatantly.

How it works

The sampler's microprocessing chip scans each waveform thousands of times per second, measuring and translating its peaks and troughs into digital information, so that it can be stored. Each individual measurement is a sample and together these thousands of separate numbers form a graph, or map, of the waveform. When they are fed back through a Digital-to-Analog Converter they are faithfully translated back into audible sound without having been electronically corrupted or distorted in any way.

Classic albums

Michael Jackson 'Thriller' (1982)

Only a genuine psychic could have foreseen the staggering transformation of Michael Jackson from Motown child star with The Jackson Five to the archetypal male megastar of the 1980s.

Michael's career had been in the doldrums after going solo at the end of the 1970s, but he was fortunate to find a mentor in the form of ace producer Quincy Jones, who gave him a complete makeover in time and in tune for the 1980s. The first flowering of that partnership was the dance/pop album 'Off The Wall' (1979) which sold over 10 million copies and delivered four smash hit singles including 'Don't Stop 'Til You Get Enough'. Although 'Off The Wall' is indisputably the better album in terms of excitement and diversity of material it was the follow-up, 'Thriller', which proved to the world how extensive and all-pervading popular music had become.

It was a strong and slickly produced album with guest appearances by Paul McCartney duetting on 'The Girl Is Mine', heavy rock guitar star Eddie Van Halen beefing up 'Beat It' and veteran horror-movie star Vincent Price giving a tongue-in-cheek monologue on the title track (something he had done a decade earlier for Alice Cooper). But the first single to be taken from it ('The Girl Is Mine') was only a top ten hit. It wasn't until the promotional video for the second single ('Beat It') broke the alleged boycott of black artists on MTV that sales soared.

Then in late 1983, 18 months after the album had been recorded, Jackson teamed up with special make-up effects expert Rick Baker and movie director John Landis (maker of the spoof horror movie *An American Werewolf in London*) to produce a visually stunning 14-minute video to promote the title track. The video became a phenomenon in itself with saturation coverage on every television station on Earth and a best-seller status of its own when commercially released the following year. Consequently the album received yet another boost and went on to sell in excess of 60 million copies worldwide.

With this one Michael Jackson made pop into a global, multicultural phenomenon. Even rumours of his eccentric behaviour and the sensationalistic publicity which surrounded allegations of sexual misconduct with a 13-year-old boy failed to put the brake on his accelerating success.

Until the release of 'Thriller' MTV had been perceived as a luxury toy for affluent white male rock adults, but afterwards every teenage rock fan wanted 24-hour rock and pop television on tap. Music television swiftly superseded rock radio as the prime listening source for new music, promo videos became as significant a factor in a record's success as the music itself (some critics might say more so), and stars were considered to have made it only when their videos were 'in heavy rotation' on MTV. It is for initiating these significant changes that Michael Jackson is likely to be remembered far into the twenty-first century, rather than for his music.

Ten essential CDs

1 Pet Shop Boys 'Discography'
2 Joy Division 'Closer'
3 New Order 'Low Life'

4 Kraftwerk 'The Man Machine'

5 OMD 'Dazzle Ships'

6 Madonna 'The Immaculate Collection'

7 Michael Jackson 'Thriller'

8 Prince 'The Hits'

9 Various Artists 'The Best Rap Album In The World … Ever'

10 The Beastie Boys 'License To III'

11 | DON'T LOOK BACK IN ANGER – BRIT-POP – THE 1990S

The 1990s witnessed a further fragmentation of popular music into an ever increasing confusion of subcategories that defied anyone over 30 to classify them. The decade began with the continuing dominance of anonymous dance music in the singles chart fortified by a new intake of identi-kit 'boy bands' and 'girl power' pop puppets manufactured and marketed to please the pre-teens. Then as if to challenge this sad state of affairs a new wave of guitar bands swept in first from Seattle and then from Britain to signal the return of what the bands and their fans saw as 'real music'. The American variety, epitomized by Nirvana, was harder and owed more to punk than pop, while the British contingent led by Suede, Blur and Oasis revived the pop sensibilities of the 1960s and 1970s. Some of the more cynical observers called this return to past values 'retro rock', but in 'cool Britannia', as it was known, it felt more like a renaissance.

Soundbite: Nirvana 'Smells Like Teen Spirit' (1991)

In the bleak, bitter winter of 1991 the smouldering intensity of Nirvana's first global hit lit a fire in the hearts of many who feared that rock music had become a corporate conveyer-belt commodity. It was one of those rare songs that stopped you in your tracks and kept you glued to the television or the radio until the last note had faded. What makes it even more poignant is the knowledge that its creator, Kurt Cobain, was to commit suicide only three years later at the height of his fame, aged 27.

Nirvana were prime purveyors of what became known as grunge, a thick wedge of sound that married garage rock, hardcore punk and heavy metal trash. Although ironically by the time Nirvana broke through, other prime exponents of the Seattle sound, including Mudhoney, Dinosaur Jr, Soundgarden, Sonic Youth, Husker Du, the Meat Puppets and the Pixies, were getting restless to move on before grunge became a fashion accessory.

However, for the unsuspecting rock fan 'Smells Like Teen Spirit' was little short of a revelation. The focus of the track is a mesmerizing mantra-like chorus wedged between a wall of heavily distorted 'fuzz' guitars and a spacious bass and drum figure over which Cobain's raw, throaty vocal vainly attempts to express crippling alienation and disillusionment. Unlike conventional rock songs it doesn't build or ride on a riff, but adopts the scissors-and-paste method of punk visuals with an all-out trash intro, falling back for a vocal verse with subdued backing from bass, drums and spacious flanged guitar. Then the mantra-like hook ('hello, hello, hello') leads into a fury of over-driven guitars which kick like wild horses before all hell breaks loose as Kurbain shreds what's left of his vocal chords on the chorus.

In one three-minute rage Nirvana rendered a roster of stadium rock acts irrelevant and redundant. The survivors merely mark time until the next Nirvana emerge to 'entertain us'.

World fusion – the future of pop?
Loop Guru/Fun^Da^Mental/Trans-Global Underground

The most exciting development in pop during the 1990s besides Brit-pop has been the emergence of the dance form 'world fusion' – an invigorating mix of multi-ethnic influences, rap and techno nurtured by young, mainly Asian artists in the cultish atmosphere of the British club circuit.

Bands such as Trans-Global Underground believe that most people are missing out on what world music has to offer and they want to introduce a wider audience to it by feeding them little snatches sweetened by a dance beat.

Musical nomads Loop Guru have the largest library of world music in the West and have been integrating it into their own music for the

last ten years. Fun^Da^Mental have been described as the Asian
Public Enemy, while TGU tend to mix Afro-Arabic and Asian
influences with acid house.

Originally formed by four young Asians, Fun^Da^Mental added
West Indian DJ and raga rapper Bad-Sha Lallaman, who raps and
toasts in Punjabi and English; Indian tabla player, percussionist and
co-vocalist Goldfinger Man-Tharoo; turntable techno-wizard DJ
Blacka Dee and founder Propa-Gandhi (aka Aki Nawaz). Their
intention was, and continues to be, the highlighting of traditional
Asian elements incorporated into hardcore rap and raga, 'whilst
promoting the beauty of Islam, Sikhism and Hinduism as well as an
anti-west (sic) political oration'. To achieve the latter they utilize
excerpts from the speeches of Malcolm X, Nelson Mandela and
Mahatma Gandhi among others.

Loop Guru have no such political ambitions, however, preferring to
weave a soft-focus, trance-inducing mantra to call the faithful to
worship at the temple of dance. For Jamud and Salman sampling is
not stealing but recycling. Everything they use, they use with
respect. While Loop Guru distanced themselves from the dance-
floor ethos, Trans-Global Underground embraced it enthusiastically,
believing that they could put cultural barriers into meltdown
through the medium of dance. It was Trans-Global's 'Temple
Head' single which first brought world fusion to the attention of the
media and, inevitably, the major record companies.

TGU are a loose collective of Arabic and Asian vocalists, keyboard
maestros and sample freaks, plus rapper Neil Sparkes thrown in for
good measure. In performance they sport exotic tribal masks, with
the exception of Indian singer and bellydancer Natasha Atlas, and
offer an exotic hybrid of dub, house, rap and roots. 'Temple Head'
peppered Tahitian chants with Burundi drums, while other tracks
on their debut album 'Dream Of 100 Nations' added zenana drones
and Indian harmoniums, fermented in an intoxicating cocktail of
cross-cultural styles.

Admittedly, this fusion of East and West has its critics – those who
would like to see traditional roots music preserved behind glass like
a precious cultural icon. But world fusion cannot be fossilized like
folk music. It could well be the future of pop for its potential is
endless.

Classic albums

Trans-Global Underground 'Dream Of 100 Nations' (1993)

Run devils and demons – TGU's debut is destined to dominate dance floors across the nation for many decades to come. For the unenlightened suffice it to say that TGU invoke a mesmerizing melange of exotic sounds, shimmering guitars, chants, atmospheric keyboards and authentic Eastern instruments, augmented by the Arabic vocals of siren Natasha Atlas and peppered with assorted percussion. After entrancing the hardcore clubbers with their novelty cult hit 'Temple Head' (included here), the band could simply have plundered the archives for more ethnic samples and grafted on a dance beat, but instead they have proven restlessly energetic in pursuit of their own material. They use samples to spice up a track, rather than as a mere substitute for their own melodic input. The result is an incomparable synthesis of acid house and ethnic influences. Full of Eastern promise. A classic by anyone's definition.

Loop Guru 'Duniya' (1994)

Those nomadic and ever-experimental global gurus, Salman and Jamud, have gone for the more club-dance-orientated sound on this, their debut album, leaving their more ambient pieces for live gigs. A wise choice, for here are 12 mind-expanding mantras, guaranteed to please both the sober world music fraternity and the club-culture tribes.

Most tracks are mid-tempo, chill-out classics, spinning around a central axis of percussion and laced with an exotic array of traditional and electric instruments, including the cora, an obligatory sitar, gamelan instruments, guitar, bass and samplers. Even the band's home-made percussion monster, which consists of hip-replacement joints, metal cogs and dustbin lids, gets a look in!

The album was a long time in the making, with the group resorting to Brian Eno's system of 'Choice Cards' whenever the options became too numerous, or a disagreement arose. Eno's 'save-a-session' system comprises 100 cards featuring instructions such as 'Reverse It', 'Do What Your Best Friend Would Do' and 'Be As Minimal As Possible', all of which seem to have been taken to heart by the intrepid duo.

Plundering their own vast private vault of field recordings, Salman and Jamud have been quietly defining and refining that most exciting hybrid 'global house', and this miniature masterpiece is the result.

These atmospheric tracks pulse with a swirling sensuality, focused around the vocal antics of Iranian exile Sussan Deihem, and spiked with pattering tablas, sampled snippets and drones. A richly textured magic-carpet ride.

REM 'Automatic For The People' (1992)

REM crept up upon an unsuspecting public as stealthily as their understated anthem 'Everybody Hurts'. In the 1980s they were just another melodic guitar band from small-town USA (Athens, Georgia, to be precise) and hopelessly unfashionable in an era dominated by dandified electronic dance acts and derivative rock revivalists. While other groups made grand empty gestures REM worked quietly on their songs, nurturing a following and the crucial support of American college radio.

When they finally broke into the big league, almost a decade after making their debut album, they had done it without compromising; the market had come to the prophet for a change. REM are a band that cannot easily be categorized although the one constant factor is their disarming simplicity. 'Automatic' is recognized as being their finest hour, but all of their albums are first and foremost collections of exquisitely crafted songs unadultered by elaborate production techniques. 'Automatic' is distinguished by being the most acoustic and intimate in their catalogue and it boasts two of their essential items, 'Man On The Moon' and 'Everybody Hurts'. Indispensable.

Oasis '(What's The Story) Morning Glory?' (1995)

In Britain in the summer of 1995 the topic of the season was not, for once, the marital machinations of the British Royal Family, but the relative merits of Brit-pop guitar bands Blur and Oasis, so much so that it became a running joke in many a comedian's routine. It is unlikely that there was anyone in Britain that year who did not at least know the name of the country's leading chart contenders, even if they hadn't actually heard their singles. It was an extraordinary time and one which can only be compared to the heyday of The Beatles and The Stones. Whether the music of Blur and Oasis will ultimately stand comparison with their 1960s heroes only time will tell, but the big question has at least been resolved. Within two years of the great debate Oasis had consolidated their success with two multimillion selling albums and a number of chart topping singles while Blur became merely interesting.

Oasis's first album, 'Definitely Maybe' (1994), had been greeted by the rock press as the most fully realized debut for decades, but was casually brushed aside by singer Liam Gallagher who declared, 'That's nothing, our kid's got 200 more [songs] just as good!'

Liam's faith in his brother Noel (the other half of the creative partnership) was borne out by the appearance of the follow-up, 'What's The Story' which exuded the same self-confident swagger and bristled with good tunes, even if some of them sounded more than vaguely familiar. The Gallaghers' debt to The Beatles is undeniable, not only in their songwriting style and Liam's Lennonesque phrasing and intonation, but also in the incidental detail such as the string arrangements which recall the post-Pepper classic 'I Am The Walrus'. Incidentally, their Beatles obsession was to culminate with Noel's duet with fellow Beatles fan Paul Weller on a cover version of 'Come Together' on a charity album, 'Help', under the auspices of Paul McCartney.

But for the 6 million plus fans who owned 'What's The Story' by the end of that extraordinary year all comparisons were academic. They knew they owned one of the most indispensable albums of the decade.

Suede 'Coming Up' (1996)

Great things were expected of retro-pop band Suede who secured the front page of British music weekly *Melody Maker* before they had even made their first record and who then went on to win the Mercury Music Prize in 1993 with their eponymously titled debut album. As the vanguard of the Brit-pop brat pack Suede were seen as the Bowie clones while Blur resurrected The Kinks and Oasis recreated The Beatles for the digital decade. The group's second album, 'Dog Man Star' (1994), was more contemporary sounding and substantially more ambitious than its predecessor and all the omens augured well for a long and illustrious career. But during the recording guitarist and co-writer Bernard Butler left the band, after which it was widely expected that Suede would disintegrate. However, contrary to all expectations, singer and writer Brett Anderson found a worthy replacement in 17-year-old Richard Oakes and the regenerated band returned with 'Coming Up', their most accomplished statement to date.

For those who remain uncharmed by the self-consciously clever Blur and Oasis's unashamed plundering of the past, Suede promise to recycle past glories into gleaming new anthems for a generation that feared all the good tunes had been written. It's true that there are strong echoes of Bowie, Bolan and Roxy Music in several tracks, specifically in 'Trash', 'Down To The Sea', 'The Beautiful Ones' and 'Saturday Night', but these are echoes rather than blatant rip-offs.

'Coming Up' presents an embarrassment of riches, one eminently hummable tune after another ornamented with memorable guitar and keyboard hooks that get under your skin and nag to be replayed.

In an era when many mainstream chart acts can be summed up by a single song, every Suede album justifies its place in a serious CD collection. If that's retro, let's have more of it!

Garbage 'Garbage' (1995)

On first hearing, Wisconsin quartet Garbage appear to be as far removed from traditional mainstream rock as it is possible to imagine and yet, there is something strangely familiar in their steam-hammer sound with its patchwork of techno, grunge and goth elements. The band was the creation of Nirvana producer Brian Vig who was able to combine techno and traditional rock to create a style with the broadcast possible appeal whilst sounding like an antidote to the retrorock brigade. But this masterstroke was recruiting vocalist Shirley Manson whose deadpan delivery and black humour gave their poppier tracks a dark, tortured tint. This, their debut album contains three hit singles ('Queer', 'Only Happens When It Rains' and 'Stupid Girl'), plus nine tracks that would have guaranteed nine more had they seen fit to release them. Flawless.

Ten essential CDs

1 The Orb 'UFOorb'
2 Nirvana 'Nevermind'
3 REM 'Automatic For The People'
4 Oasis '(What's The Story) Morning Glory'
5 Suede 'Coming Up'
6 Garbage 'Garbage'
7 Trans-Global Underground 'Dream Of 100 Nations'
8 Loop Guru 'Duniya'
9 Primal Scream 'Screamadelica'
10 Blur 'Parklife'

12 | REELIN' AND ROCKIN' – ROCK ON FILM

A printed history of rock and pop can convey only a proportion of the music's appeal. Even listening to the records themselves doesn't tell the whole story. The real acid test for a performer is, of course, the live concert, but many of the legends of rock have passed on or passed their prime, so for the fan the next best thing is to watch them strutting their stuff on the small screen.

The 1950s

During the 1950s and early 1960s the American and European film industry cynically exploited what the studio executives would have called the burgeoning 'teen market'. In less than a decade they had churned out dozens of low-budget formula 'rock-and-roll' flicks in which performances by both genuine rock stars and second-rate novelty acts were tenuously linked by a storyline so banal that it was ripe for parody even before the genre was properly established. Some of the early exploitation items have since attained cult status for their kitsch appeal, but the majority are of little interest other than for the musical performances that they preserved.

Blackboard Jungle (1955) has a serious claim on being the first genuine rock-and-roll movie, although it did not actually put any rock stars on the screen. It was a gritty melodrama about a vocational school teacher (Glenn Ford) struggling to gain control and respect from a class of delinquents, but it packed in the Teddy Boys wherever it played because producer Pandro S Berman had the foresight to feature Bill Haley's 'Rock Around The Clock' behind the opening credits. The inclusion of the song guaranteed full houses and ripped cinema seats wherever movie-house managers were brave enough to book it.

The resulting publicity and potential for profit was not lost on the prolific B-movie producer Sam Katzman who lost no time in hustling Bill Haley into a movie of his own. *Rock Around the Clock* (1956) featuring Haley, Little Richard and The Platters was pure teen fodder, a cheap-and-cheerful second feature hung on a slender storyline concerning the discovery of a band playing a new form of jive. It was a hackneyed showbusiness rags-to-riches story and typical of the time, but it established a new genre almost overnight – the rock movie.

Other flicks followed in quick succession for fear that the new fad might fade before the studios had a chance to cash in. *Don't Knock the Rock* (1956) the sequel to *Rock Around the Clock*, was rushed out in the same year and again featured Bill Haley; *High School Confidential* (1958) boasted Jerry Lee Lewis; *Go Johnny Go* (1959) had Richie Valens, Eddie Cochran, The Cadillacs, The Flamingos and Chuck Berry, while Berry cropped up again in *Mr Rock and Roll* (1957).

Although it was by far the best of the bunch, the Jayne Mansfield comedy vehicle *The Girl Can't Help It* (1956) scored for its self-mocking script, high production values and lush colour cinematography. It also boasted one of the strongest line-ups of rock-and-roll talent to be caught on camera, namely Little Richard, Eddie Cochran and Fats Domino. It was fun, but like the other rock movies of the era it was nothing radically new. The format and plot were warmed-over Hollywood musical clichés with the performances spliced in at random to reawaken the audience's interest whenever the action flagged.

The same can be said for the best that the British had to offer, namely a series of vacuous vehicles (*Expresso Bongo*, *The Young Ones* and *Summer Holiday*) starring the anaemic Cliff Richard, whose quivering lip exhibited more life than the cardboard characters or the soundtrack. The British attitude to pop at that time can be gleaned from the fact that its best shot was a big-screen spin-off from the television series *6.5 Special* featuring skiffle star Lonnie Donegan, pop poppet Petula Clark and Jim Dale, a talented entertainer who was later to find fame as a comic actor in the 'Carry On' films.

Elvis

Elvis Presley's early movies were in a different league with strong storylines, atmospheric cinematography, a real sense of pace and superior songs, many of them penned by hit-makers Leiber and Stoller.

Presley's first appearance was in a run-of-the-mill western originally to have been called *The Reno Brothers*, but retitled *Love Me Tender* (1956) to capitalize on his current hit single of the same name. As his confidence increased in proportion to his box-office returns he was given more demanding roles. His brooding performances in *Jailhouse Rock* (1957) and *King Creole* (1958) had been coaxed out of him by highly experienced movie directors who ensured that the King emerged with his credibility intact and his image enhanced. But his subsequent movies (of which there were more than 30) were all candyfloss and corn, carelessly and shamelessly thrown together in a desperate effort to package Presley as an all-round family entertainer.

Incredibly, Presley was the only rock idol of the 1950s to get the full Hollywood star treatment. Eddie Cochran, Gene Vincent, Jerry Lee Lewis, Little Richard and the rest had to be content with featured roles in hastily scripted and routinely shot B-movies whose plots had clearly been contrived to string together the musical numbers.

Flashbacks to the 1950s

In later decades there were indispensable film biographies of Chuck Berry (*Hail! Hail! Rock and Roll*), Elvis (*This Is Elvis*), and fictional recreations based on the lives of Jerry Lee Lewis (*Great Balls of Fire*), Buddy Holly (*The Buddy Holly Story*) and, of course, the King (*Elvis*), plus nostalgic recreations of the era (*American Hot Wax* and *American Graffiti*) which boasted soundtracks bristling with dozens of essential 1950s classics. Director George Lucas made such a good job of bringing back to life the cruising culture of small-town America in the 1950s in *American Graffiti* (1973) that the film sparked a genuine rock-and-roll revival.

The 1960s

The Beatles

It was perhaps inevitable that The Beatles would shake up the movies once they got around to making films, just as they had woken up the music business with their energy and infectious enthusiasm. Fortunately, when the moment came for them to make the move to the big screen they were entrusted to a director who realized that the group's biggest assets were their naturalness and dry Liverpudlian humour.

For their first and arguably their best outing *A Hard Day's Night* (1964), director Richard Lester opted for a pseudo-documentary style which allowed the Fab Four to be themselves, using the genuinely amusing Alan Owen screenplay as a springboard for their own gags. The editing was as fast and as snappy as the songs, which were an integral element of the story rather than being merely decorative.

The Beatles' second movie, *Help!* (1965), was a crushing disappointment in comparison. Whereas the first film was fast and funny, the second was merely frantic and clearly trying desperately to be different. By this time the band were world famous and under great pressure to exceed their fans' expectations with the result that the film looked like a big-budget home movie that was clearly fun to make, but rather tiresome for those who had sit through the bits in between the songs.

Much more fun was the full-length animation fantasy, *Yellow Submarine* (1968), which was not actually their movie, although you wouldn't know it as it featured the Fab Four as cartoon characters with their voices dubbed by impersonators. Even so, it did healthy box-office business and it went some way towards winning back the goodwill the band had lost through the self-indulgent psychedelic television travelogue *Magical Mystery Tour* (1967). Ironically, although the latter was severely criticized at the time, in retrospect it looks like an unedited experimental pop video which might not have appeared so aimless had someone been given the opportunity to cut it down to size.

The Beatles' final film, *Let It Be* (1970), was planned as a *Hard Days Night*-type documentary whose fly-on-the-wall approach would capture the group as they rehearsed for a back-to-basics album. As it turned out, it captured them coming apart at the seams, but is compelling viewing. The final sequence with the band playing together on the roof of the recording studio, giving it all they've got as if they knew it was their last live performance, is one of the great moments in cinema, as well as in rock. 'I'd like to thank you all on behalf of the band,' says Lennon dryly as they're escorted from the roof by the police, 'and I hope we passed the audition.'

Prior to the release of the Beatles' *Anthology*, an eight-volume video collection, the definitive documentary had been *The Complete Beatles*, which remains one of the most comprehensive and intelligent documentaries to date. The most accurate recreation of their early years was to be seen in *Backbeat* (1980), in which the group were portrayed by other musicians who not only got into character, but managed to recreate the sound and spirit of the period so well that it succeeds as a movie on its own terms.

Mud and music – 1960s concert films

For those who wanted their rock in the raw, as it were, *Monterey Pop* (1968) was the first and best of the plethora of 1960s 'concert films' which brought the mud and music to fans who could never hope to travel to the sites of the great rock festivals.

New lightweight 16mm cameras gave director D A Pennebaker and his crew the freedom to flit about in the wings, zooming in for remarkable close-ups. But Pennebaker couldn't restrain his crew's enthusiasm for their new toys, with the result that many unrepeatable performances were ruined by excessive visual trickery. Monterey proved to the world that it was possible for several hundred thousand hippies to sit in a field for three days and have nothing but a good time, and it gave many of the Bay Area bands worldwide exposure for free. Janis Joplin, previously unknown outside of California, was promptly signed by Columbia Records; while Jefferson Airplane, Country Joe and The Fish and Canned Heat found themselves big names overnight.

But it wasn't all peace and good vibes. Pennebaker's movie gives no indication of the wrangling that went on behind the scenes between the idealistic San Francisco bands such as The Grateful Dead and the LA business-orientated promoters. The Dead wanted Monterey to be a free festival, and when they didn't get their way they refused permission for their performance to be filmed, ending up playing for free in a football field a couple of miles down the road.

Although Jimi Hendrix had established himself in Britain by this point, he was virtually unknown in his native America before taking the stage at Monterey (on Paul McCartney's insistence). Jimi's set is undoubtedly the highlight of the movie, though The Who run a close second with a devastating version of 'My Generation', complete with ritualistic amp and guitar destruction. Hendrix countered by playing his axe with his teeth, before finally setting it ablaze with lighter fuel to the obvious bemusement of the audience.

As a film *Monterey Pop* has considerable technical failings and has dated rather badly, but as a visual record of these legendary performers it remains essential viewing.

If *Monterey Pop* celebrated the birth of the hippy era with admirable economy and with the bands firmly in focus, then *Woodstock* (1970) documented its inevitable demise in a rambling three-hour feature centring on the most famous festival of them all.

Director Michael Wadleigh was astute enough to realize that the half-a-million strong crowd were as much a part of the event as the bands they had come to see. He caught them tripping, dancing, rolling in the mud and soaking up the upper New York state sunshine before focusing on the traffic jams, the lack of food and sanitation, the births and deaths, the dope dealers and the garbage which resulted from 'the largest group of people ever to have assembled in one place'.

Among those who played that August weekend back in 1969 and who subsequently made it on to celluloid were Canned Heat, Joe Cocker, The Who, Ten Years After, Santana and Jimi Hendrix. The last named is seen torturing the 'Star Spangled Banner' to great effect at 9:30 a.m. on the Monday morning watched by a paltry 30,000 people and an army of litter gatherers. A poignant finale if ever there was one.

Other 1960s acts to make it on to celluloid included lightweight pop puppets The Monkees (*Head*), heavyweights Cream (*Cream's Farewell Concert*) and the stalwarts of the 1960s Jethro Tull, The Who and The Rolling Stones (*Rock and Roll Circus*).

The 1970s

Hendrix

An unintentional footnote to *Woodstock* occurs during *Jimi Hendrix Plays Berkeley* (1971), in which hippies are seen demonstrating outside a cinema where *Woodstock* is playing. 'You can't charge us $3.50 for a ticket,' yells one of the protesters, '*we* made that film!' The remaining half an hour or so is then given over to Jimi's set at Berkeley University, which includes a manic version of 'Voodoo Chile' plus assured performances of 'Johnny B Goode', 'Purple Haze', 'Pass It On' and 'Machine Gun'. But as with many of these low-budget documentaries, the hand-held camera work is often erratic, allowing Jimi to weave in and out of the frame and a blinding spotlight to beam straight into the lens.

Hendrix was not well served by the film industry during his lifetime, being too trusting and allowing spaced-out wackos to use footage of his gigs in pretentious drivel such as *Rainbow Bridge* (1971). For the first 45 minutes *Bridge* is a meandering psychic travelogue of Hawaii and a look at a psychic commune whose members are waiting for visitors from Venus! The assorted weirdos had obviously partaken of too many acid drops, and judging by the use of Second World War footage(!) so had the director! Howl in disbelief as one hippy mumbles: 'I got rid of my wizard's hat because ... you don't need a leader!'

Most of the characters in this amateur home movie are more 'laid out' than 'laid back', with Jimi so 'far out' of the frame that he does not even appear until his staged open-air gig at the end. But his short set almost makes up for the aimless dross that precedes it as he thunders through 'Hear My Train A Coming', 'Purple Haze' and a superior version of 'Voodoo Chile'. He may have been one of rock's innovators and *the* greatest guitarist in the history of popular music but, as *Rainbow Bridge* shows only too well, he also made a number of bum career moves.

It was left to record producer Joe Boyd to put Jimi's career into perspective. His carefully compiled retrospective, simply titled *Jimi Hendrix* (1973), featured 11 tracks culled from various film and television appearances and augmented with interviews with Pete Townshend, Mick Jagger, Lou Reed and Eric Clapton. Some of the musical sequences are unavailable elsewhere, making this a film not to be missed.

The Stones on celluloid

The heady optimism which characterized the late 1960s came to a sudden and brutal end at the Altamont Speedway just four months after Woodstock.

The Rolling Stones planned to climax their 1969 US tour with a free one-day festival at the site, supported by several Bay Area bands: Santana, The Grateful Dead and Jefferson Airplane. Then someone in the Stones' camp had the bright idea of deputizing a local chapter of the Hells Angels to act as security, a way of showing that the 'love generation' could police itself – it proved to be a fatal mistake.

The 'Angels' quarrelled first with the bands and then the zonked-out crowd, and finally – after being whipped into a frenzy by Jagger during 'Sympathy For The Devil' – one of their number stabbed a black youth to death as he approached the stage armed with a revolver. For all their posturing, The Stones were seen to be helpless when confronted with real violence. Sadly, *Gimme Shelter* (1971), the film of the tour, becomes less of a 'rockumentary' and more of a murder preceded by music.

Ironically, it's a film which otherwise enhances the band's reputation. Much of the footage preceding 'the incident' and its aftermath shows The Stones at their best. An early segment taken from their performance at Madison Square Garden is particularly compelling, with sound supervised by Glyn Johns and inspired camera work by Albert and David Maysles. The Stones have seldom been photographed to better advantage. Even their glossy, quadraphonic concert film *Ladies and Gentlemen, The Rolling Stones* (1974), which offered 14 uninterrupted tracks from their 1972 US tour and Hal Ashby's record of their 1981 tour, *Let's Spend the Night Together*, failed to match the primeval power of *Gimme Shelter*.

1970s concert films

By the early 1970s artists and film-makers were eager to follow the example set by *Monterey Pop* and *Woodstock*. Anyone who could afford a camera and could blag their way backstage was passing themselves off as a director. It was a liggers' paradise, where self-indulgent, incoherent, tricked-up home movies were touted as high art. Occasionally, though, the documentary approach worked very well, blurring the divide between stage and screen although few film-makers could recapture the atmosphere of a live rock concert. But as the stars became shrewder and more media aware they manipulated the movies for their own ends, using film techniques to add to their own mystique, and distancing themselves still further from their audience. Dylan, for example, had persuaded the ubiquitous D A Pennebaker to excise footage from *Don't Look Back* (1967) in order to eliminate the scenes which showed him talking openly to his fans. David Bowie went one better and pulled the plug on Pennebaker's film of his final performance as Ziggy Stardust in 1972. *Ziggy Stardust – The Movie* was shelved for 12 years and then dusted off for video, by which time Bowie's futuristic floor show looked decidedly dated.

The entertainment industry as a whole was in poor shape by the mid-1970s with nostalgia being the only area of growth. *That'll Be the Day* (1973) recreated the stifling atmosphere of Britain in the 1950s with gritty realism and an evocative soundtrack. Its sequel, *Stardust* (1974), brought the story up to date as its central character (played by David Essex) turned his back on the provinces for pop stardom only to be suffocated by the pressures of success.

There were also movie revivals of rock musicals which had proved successful on stage (*Hair*, *Jesus Christ Superstar*, *Godspell* and *Grease*), but with the exception of the last named these failed to transfer to the big screen.

Low-budget 'tour movies' seemed the ideal answer. Their production cost was minimal but the return, if reflected by the artist's popularity, could be considerable. Among those who succumbed to the lure of the big screen were Marc Bolan (*Born to Boogie*, 1972), Pink Floyd (*Live at Pompeii*, 1971), ELP (*Pictures at an Exhibition*, 1972), Yes (*Yessongs*, 1975), Led Zeppelin (*The*

Song Remains the Same, 1976), Genesis (*A Band in Concert*, 1976) and continuing the tradition into the 1980s were The Clash (*Rude Boy*, 1980), AC/DC (*Let There Be Rock*, 1980), Black Sabbath and Blue Öyster Cult (*Black and Blue*, 1980), Van Morrison (*In Ireland*, 1980), Eric Clapton (*E C and his Rolling Hotel*, 1980) and Talking Heads (*Stop Making Sense*, 1983). In addition there were superstar sessions such as *The Concert for Bangladesh* (1972) featuring George Harrison, Eric Clapton, Bob Dylan and chums and Martin Scorsese's record of The Band's farewell bash, *The Last Waltz* (1978).

Some of these have a grainy look, being videotape-to-film transfers, with little or no exposition; just a record of a performance which you saw if you were a fan or avoided if you weren't. A couple have since surfaced on video, but the majority remain a reminder of the amateur enthusiasm that characterized rock movies in the pre-MTV and video era.

Rock as soundtrack

Prior to the late 1960s sales of film soundtrack albums were thought to be limited to film buffs, but both the film and music industries woke up to the potential benefits of trailing a new movie with a hit song with the phenomenal success of the James Bond films, whose creators hired high-calibre pop performers to sing the main theme to each of their new releases. Over the years these reflected the changing trends in pop, from Tom Jones in the 1960s and Paul McCartney in the 1970s to Duran Duran in the 1980s.

Easy Rider (1969) is widely regarded as the first film to use rock as a dramatic score, although the previous year Richard Rush had included tracks by Cream and Iron Butterfly in his minor motorcycle odyssey *The Savage Seven*. Until then film producers had been reluctant to use previously released material on the soundtrack, as the legal problems and royalty agreements had been formidable. But *Easy Rider* showed it was possible, and proved it to be very profitable both for the film-makers and the record companies who licensed the tracks. The soundtrack album, which included 'The Pusher' and 'Born To Be Wild' by Steppenwolf, 'If Six Was Nine' by Jimi Hendrix and 'The Weight' by The Band, sold phenomenally well and led to a queue of A and R men outside the production offices of every major studio in Hollywood.

Records were then used to sell cinema tickets, and movies in turn helped to sell records – a strategy which has since become common practice in the entertainment industry. Sometimes the artist might appear on screen, as did Bob Dylan (in *Pat Garrett and Billy The Kid*), Whitney Houston (in *The Bodyguard*) and rapper Ice-T (in *New Jack City*). Or they might supply the main song and in return have access to clips to enhance their video as did Queen in *Highlander* and *Flash Gordon* and rapper Coolio who used scenes from the movie *Dangerous Minds* (an updating of *Blackboard Jungle*) to promote the global hit 'Gangsta's Paradise'. Other artists found themselves unexpectedly back in fashion after their old hits were featured in a hit movie. *Trainspotting* resurrected the career of Lou Reed, *The Full Monty* revived the fortunes of Errol Brown of Hot Chocolate, while *Four Weddings and a Funeral* made a fortune for forgotten 1960s rocker Reg Presley of The Troggs when his song 'Love Is All Around' was featured in a cover version by boy band Wet Wet Wet.

By the 1990s every Hollywood studio would underwrite the risk of its investment by featuring pop songs on the soundtrack and pop artists would see the attendant publicity as free promotion for their songs. It became irrelevant whether tracks by Prince and U2, for example, contributed to the plot of *Batman Forever* (1997), or whether Celine Dion's melodramatic ballad 'My Heart Will Go On' was in keeping with the period setting of *Titanic* (1998). Music had become merely an element in the marketing equation. But in *Easy Rider* the score was integral to the plot, furthering the story and giving voice to emotions and thoughts which it would have been difficult for the characters to express through dialogue.

The music of 1970s soul stars Isaac Hayes, Curtis Mayfield and Marvin Gaye served a very different purpose in a series of superspade movies (*Shaft*, *Superfly* and *Trouble Man*) that collectively gave impetus to a new sub-genre known as blaxploitation films. The tracks served the same purpose as John Barry's James Bond theme, as a reminder that no matter what was happening on screen the black detective was in control, that he dictated the pace and that everyone else moved to his rhythm. The soundtrack albums to these films are still steady sellers more than 30 years on and are as valid as any of the artists' studio albums. The first reggae film, *The Harder They Come* (1972), featuring Jimmy Cliff was of a similar type, but as with the blaxploitation films it is the soundtrack album that is worth hunting down, not a print of the movie.

Rock musicals

If the concert films made it to your local cinema it is likely that they would have been as supporting features to those late-night 'revival house' favourites *Phantom of the Paradise* (1974), *The Rocky Horror Picture Show* (1975) and *Tommy* (1975).

Phantom, directed by Brian De Palma, was a colourful remake of the *Phantom of the Opera* with Paul Williams as a dwarfish rock promoter and a clutch of original songs sung by the cast. Despite its director's characteristic over-the-top treatment, however, it didn't catch on because its humour came at the expense of the audience and it took its romantic sub-plot too seriously.

No one took *anything* seriously in Jim Sharman's deliciously wicked adaptation of the long-running theatrical hit *The Rocky Horror Picture Show* (1975), in which Tim Curry repeated his stage role as Dr Frank N Furter, the self-confessed 'sweet transvestite from transsexual Transylvania'. Meatloaf did likewise with a cameo appearance as Eddie the Neanderthal rocker, while Susan Sarandon and Barry Bostwick played Janet and Brad, the straightlaced suburban couple who chance upon the weirdo's castle after their car breaks down. Much of the movie's gaudy charm is lost unless you can see it in the company of its die-hard fans who turn each screening of this camp horror musical into a bizarre party – dressing up like their favourite character, reciting the entire script from memory and singing along with the songs. *Rocky Horror* is *the* cult movie of all time, currently playing every Friday and Saturday night in 200 cinemas across the United States.

Ken Russell's *Tommy* (1975) was an equally garish, stunning and occasionally surreal visual barrage which suited the operatic material extremely well, but it lacked *Rocky Horror*'s self-effacing charm.

Roger Daltrey made a convincing deaf, dumb and blind 'boy', Elton John provided light relief as his pinball rival, Tina Turner made the Acid Queen her own and Ann-Margret earned herself an Academy Award nomination as Tommy's long-suffering mother. Others appearing included the late Oliver Reed, Jack Nicholson, Paul Nicholas, Eric Clapton, Arthur Brown and, of course, the 'orrible 'Oo themselves. Pete Townshend, however, wrote only one song specifically for the movie version, 'Champagne' – sung by Ann-Margret as she writhed around in a sea of baked beans!

Punk

Punk came and went before the movie industry could capture it on film, although the ever enterprising Malcolm McLaren made sure that his boys made the big screen, even if he had to use old footage to pad it out as the band had split during shooting. *The Great Rock 'N' Roll Swindle* (1978) mimicked the style of a tacky tabloid exposé in telling the story of how the Sex Pistols hoodwinked the record industry into parting with large amount of cash, although McLaren was too engrossed in portraying himself as a latter-day Fagin to have noticed that there was more to it than that.

The sordid story of Pistols' bass player Sid Vicious and his equally ill-fated girlfriend Nancy Spunge was later unravelled in *Sid and Nancy* (1986), an ill-conceived and depressing study of drug addiction, degradation and death.

In contrast, Roger 'Quickie' Corman produced the daft but endearing *Rock and Roll High School* (1979) as a starring vehicle for The Ramones, whose image was a self-parody to begin with.

Business as usual

But just as the music industry had closed ranks to freeze out punk and intensified the marketing of more mainstream acts as if punk had never happened, so the film industry did likewise. At the end of the 1970s there was a run of dire disco movies which only served to confirm how shallow and contrived white dance music had become. In quick succession we had *Saturday Night Fever* (1977),

Thank God it's Friday (1978), *Can't Stop the Music* (1980), *Xanadu* (1980) and, by far the liveliest of the lot, *Fame* (1980), the only film in which the dancers appeared to work up a sweat.

There was no trace of exertion when Europop icons Abba went through the motions of making a film of their 1977 Australian tour whose wafer-thin plot revolved around a hapless hack trying to get an interview with the Swedish supergroup. Had they shot it a decade later as a big-budget concert video it might have been more effective, but as a docudrama *Abba – The Movie* (1978) could have pleased only their undiscerning prepubescent fans.

Quadrophenia (1979) was by contrast a grimy and realistic study of working-class youth in the mid-1960s. Phil Daniels was perfect as the Mod in search of an identity, Sting was suitably imposing as the Ace Face and every other character seemed natural and totally convincing. First-time director Franc Roddam caught the look and feel of the period perfectly, complementing tracks from The Who's double album with contemporary American records. *Quadrophenia* is one of the most exhilarating rock movies of the last 25 years and was, in part, responsible for a short-lived mod revival in Britain for which Coventry's ska specialist Two-Tone label provided the perfect soundtrack.

Having been involved both artistically and financially with *Tommy* and then *Quadrophenia*, The Who were keen to capitalize on their archive of promo clips and concert footage. *The Kids are Alright* (1979) began as a celebration of 15 years of The Who, but ultimately became a tribute to Keith Moon who died just after its completion. Essentially a random selection of clips with only brief interview extracts by way of explanation, it includes virtually every Who anthem, plus a couple of live sequences staged specially for the film, to make this *the* definitive Who retrospective.

The 1980s and 1990s

The first sign that mainstream film producers were willing to put as much into a rock production as they used to take out came as late as 1982 with Alan Parker's version of *The Wall*. Originally written as a solo project by Floyd's Roger Waters, it had burgeoned into an ambitious group 'concept' and was subsequently hailed as the zenith of Floyd's career. Its scope and subject matter, the gradual dehumanization of a fictional rock star (played by Bob Geldof) by an oppressive society, allowed Parker's imagination free reign. He mixed live action with striking animation by artist Gerald Scarfe, fantasy sequences and flashbacks which gave credence to the star's self-destructive tendencies.

The advent of the domestic video market and 24-hour pop promos on MTV in the early 1980s spelt the end of the rock movie, although there were a few valiant attempts to entice teenagers back to the cinema. *Purple Rain* (1984), *Moonwalker* (1988), *In Bed with Madonna* (1990) and *Spiceworld* (1997) were all standard star vehicles for Prince, Michael Jackson, Madonna and the Spice Girls respectively, which pleased the fans if not the critics and underlined the impression that rock movies had not really developed from the basic showbiz clichés of *Rock Around The Clock*.

More imaginative and far more entertaining were the low-budget spoof rockumentary *This Is Spinal Tap* (1983), in which every rock cliché was mercilessly lampooned, and Alan Parker's witty and perceptive drama *The Commitments* (1991). In stark contrast director Oliver Stone sank $40 million in a dour biopic of Jim Morrison, *The Doors* (1991), and succeeded only in demystifying Morrison who came across as a serious case of arrested development rather than as an icon in the making.

Video has now effectively replaced the rock movie although, ironically, many of the three-minute promos which now saturate satellite and terrestrial television day and night cost almost as much as the earlier feature films. In the final analysis the marriage of rock and the cinema was unfulfilled. All that rock fans want is a record of their favourite band in performance and video ably satisfies that need.

GLOSSARY

Album In the pre-CD era the typical Long Playing record, or LP, would be a collection of songs (some of which might have been previously released as singles) totalling approximately 40 minutes (20 minutes per side).

Blues A black American song form based on the tonic, subdominant and dominant chords (e.g. a blues in E would consist of the chords E, A and B) with minor intervals and flattened third and seventh notes in the scale frequently in a 12-bar format.

Brit-pop A revival of 1960s-styled guitar-dominated pop which came to dominate the UK music scene in the 1990s.

Country The folk music of the southern states of America with headquarters in Nashville. Previously known as Country and Western.

Crooner A romantic balladeer such as Bing Crosby, Frank Sinatra and Dean Martin popular in the 1940s and 1950s.

Disco A form of dance music popular in the 1970s in which the melodic content was generally considered to be subservient to the beat.

Doo-wop Close harmony vocal music popular in America during the 1950s which took its name from the wordless backing harmonies.

Garage rock Mid-1960s pre-psychedelic minimalist US rock movement typified by a frenetic three-chord, three-minute thrash, screaming vocals, distorted guitars and an occasional electric organ line.

Glam rock   Early 1970s initiated by Marc Bolan of T Rex and later taken to extremes by David Bowie, The Sweet and Gary Glitter which sought to put the fun and glamour back into pop. It was initially a British phenomenon aimed at a pre-teen audience.

Gospel   Black sacred music characterized by soulful bel canto-styled singing known as melisma and often structured around a liturgical call-and-response format.

Grunge   A hybrid of punk and hard rock which originated in Seattle in the early 1990s, popularized and exemplified by Nirvana.

Hard rock   A guitar driven genre which differs from heavy metal in that it is less rigid and riff orientated and frequently draws on the blues format and feel.

Heavy metal   A highly stylized form of rock which relies on a repeated riff to propel the song forward. When it first appeared in the late 1960s it drew its imagery from Sword and Sorcery fiction and horror comics.

Hillbilly   A derogatory term used to describe country music.

Hippy   Follower of the 1960s idealistic 'Flower Power' culture.

House music   Bass-heavy dance style originating in Chicago in the early 1980s. House records were a hybrid of 1970s disco music and electronics 'created' by club DJs who fed black disco and soul records from the 1970s through a computer, keyboard and drum machine.

Merseybeat   A briefly fashionable style of guitar pop which emerged from Liverpool in the wake of The Beatles' early success (c 1964/5).

Mixing   The balancing of separate tracks on which individual instruments and voices have been recorded to produce the tape from which a record will be made.

Moog   An early type of electronic syhthesizer.

Motown   1960s Detroit-based dance label with a distinctive sound deriving its name from the city's nick name, motor town. Artists included Stevie Wonder and Diana Ross.

Multi-track   A recording format which allows a number of signal sources (instruments, vocals, effects) to be recorded separately on to the same piece of tape and then played back in perfect synchronization.

New wave   A less anarchistic post-punk movement which promised to put some of the raw energy of punk into mainstream pop but instead became a catch-all term for a new generation of artists who came to prominence in the post-punk era.

Pop   A broad, catch-all term which is generally used to refer to commercial, fashion-conscious popular music as opposed to rock which is considered to be harder and uncompromising.

Pop art   A form of painting and illustration which became fashionable in the 1960s which aimed to imitate the highly stylized images in American comic books and sought inspiration in popular culture.

Progressive rock   (also known as pomp rock). A genre popular in the late 1960s and early 1970s which attempted to broaden the musical vocabulary, instrumentation and themes used by rock groups in an effort to create a hybrid of rock and classical music.

Producer   The nominally creative force behind recording sessions whose job varies between steering the artists towards creating what he (or she), the producer, wanted to hear and assisting the artist to capture what they heard in their heads.

Protest movement   1960s politicized folk music as exemplified by early Bob Dylan.

Psych-pop   Hybrid between mind-expanding psychedelia and Sixties-styled pop music (i.e. a standard format three-minute single with weird dissonant sounds and an offbeat theme as opposed to a lengthy, apparently formless, instrumental 'freak out').

Psychedelia/acid rock   Late 1960s pop whose themes and sounds sought to re-create the hallucinogenic effects of mind-expanding drugs such as LSD ('acid').

Punk   Primal minimalist rock of the mid- to late 1970s which celebrated a back-to-basics approach and anti-establishment ethic.

Rap   The dominant genre of black pop in the 1980s and 1990s, characterized by a polemic monologue delivered over an insistent dance rhythm and instrumental snippets sampled from records by other artists.

Reggae   The popular music of Jamaica with a characteristic emphasis on the off-beat.

Rhythm and Blues (R&B)   A dance-orientated form of black popular music with a strong back beat dating back to the 1940s which later formed the basis of rock and roll. Not to be confused with the bland dance form of the 1990s which adopted the same name.

Rock   A general term for popular music with a harder edge aimed at a late teens–twenties audience.

Rock and Roll   Specifically the vibrant American popular music of the mid- to late 1950s.

Rockabilly   The first expression of rock and roll to emerge from the southern United States with a strong country/hillbilly element.

Sampling   A method of digitally recording excerpts from other artists' records which can then be manipulated with special effects and replayed at key moments on an entirely new recording. In this way a favourite guitar riff or vocal phrase could add interest to a dance track that needs to be spiced up.

San Francisco Sound   Specifically the music of the Bay Area bands in the late 1960s which was not exclusively psychedelic, but echoed hippy ideals and the emerging drug culture.

Scratching   An effect similar to hearing a record stuck in the groove created by manually manipulating two adjacent turntables so that the stylus is drawn backwards through the groove.

Single   45 rpm, seven-inch record format with one song on each side. In the early years of pop the A-side featured the more commercial song while the B-side would be a throwaway 'filler'. But there were also double A sides, maxi singles (three tracks; one on the A side and two on the flip), seven-inch EPs (extended plays; four tracks) and, from the 1970s, 12-inch singles which have a wider dynamic range and superior sound. As a very general rule singles have always been the currency of commercial mass-market pop, while albums became increasingly important from the late 1960s as rock artists needed more space to express their ideas.

Ska   An early form of reggae popular with a section of the white audience (specifically the mods) in the 1960s.

Skiffle   A rough and ready amateur form of folk rock briefly popular in Britain during the late 1950s.

Soul   Black popular music blending dance rhythms and emotive gospel-style vocals.

Sun sound   The distinctive sound of early American rock and roll records associated with the Sun recording studio and label in Memphis, characterized by a long tape delay echo effect.

Supergroup   A new 'elite' group formed by artists who had previously made their reputations in other bands. A fashionable trend in the late 1960s and early 1970s.

Surfing   Early 1960s West Coast American close harmony pop preoccupied with the surfing culture as exemplified by The Beach Boys and duo Jan and Dean.

Techno   Frantic 'soul-less' computer-generated dance music originating in Detroit in the late 1980s.

World fusion   An exotic blend of world music (traditional folk music) and rock usually combining ethnic and rock instrumentation to create dance music with cross-cultural appeal.

INDEX

TEACH YOURSELF

CLASSICAL MUSIC

Stephen Collins

Clear and concise yet comprehensive, this book provides a practical introduction to the world of classical music for the newcomer. Stephen Collins takes the listening experience as the starting point, and fills in factual details along the way. New topics are introduced step by step, and are always presented from the listener's point of view. These include:

- listening to music: developing skills
- what is classical music?
- the architecture of music: forms and structures
- historical background: different periods and different styles
- the instruments of the orchestra
- starting a collection of recorded music

Examples from well-known pieces are examined in a clear and non-technical way. Whether you dip into *Teach Yourself Classical Music* from time to time, or read it straight through, you will feel that your musical horizons have been broadened, and that you have gained the knowledge and confidence to extend your musical experiences further.

Stephen Collins has played and taught music for over twenty years. He is currently a WEA tutor, and works for a major publishing company.

Other related titles

TEACH YOURSELF

JAZZ

Rodney Dale

Teach Yourself Jazz offers something for everyone whose imagination has been captured by the exciting world of jazz. The book looks at the origins and developments of jazz, and gives insight into its musical structures and the way in which it is played. It is an essential guide for both the beginner and the more experienced musician or listener.

Teach Yourself Jazz introduces the music from a number of angles, including:

- its musical and cultural history
- its musical structure
- the instruments upon which it is played
- important practitioners and bands

Whether you read the book from cover to cover, or dip into it for specific information, it will help you improve your understanding, appreciation, and enjoyment of the music and its culture.

Rodney Dale has been involved with jazz for over 40 years, including playing piano with a number of bands, organizing classes and workshops on jazz appreciation, and writing books on the subject.

Other related titles

MUSIC

King Palmer

This book provides a concise introduction and reference guide to the theory, practice and history of music.

The making of music with different instruments, including the singing voice, and the principles of musical notation, scales, melody and harmony are examined, followed by advice on how to practice. King Palmer describes the range and repertoire of the keyboard, stringed, woodwind, brass and percussion families and explains how they come together in the modern orchestra. He then traces the development of music, from its early forms to the great periods of classical, romantic and modern composition, alongside traditional, ethnic, popular and electronic forms.

Teach Yourself Music is an invaluable guide for students, and offers new insights to all those who take pleasure in making or listening to music.